Biblical Management Principles

HARVESTIME INTERNATIONAL INSTITUTE

This course is part of the **Harvestime International Institute**, a program designed to equip believers for effective spiritual harvest.

The basic theme of the training is to teach what Jesus taught, that which took men who were fishermen, tax collectors, etc., and changed them into reproductive Christians who reached their world with the Gospel in a demonstration of power.

This manual is a single course in one of several modules of curriculum which moves believers from visualizing through deputizing, multiplying, organizing, and mobilizing to achieve the goal of evangelizing.

TABLE OF CONTENTS

HOW TO USE THIS MANUAL

MANUAL FORMAT

Each lesson consists of:

Objectives: These are the goals you should achieve by studying the chapter. Read them before starting the lesson.

Key Verse: This verse emphasizes the main concept of the chapter. Memorize it.

Chapter Content: Study each section. Use your Bible to look up any references not printed in the manual.

Self-Test: Take this test after you finish studying the chapter. Try to answer the questions without using your Bible or this manual. When you have concluded the Self-Test, check your answers in the answer section provided at the end of the book.

For Further Study: This section will help you continue your study of the Word of God, improve your study skills, and apply what you have learned to your life and ministry.

Final Examination: If you are enrolled in this course for credit, you received a final examination along with this course. Upon conclusion of this course, you should complete this examination and return it for grading as instructed.

ADDITIONAL MATERIALS NEEDED

You will need a King James version of the Bible.

SUGGESTIONS FOR GROUP STUDY

FIRST MEETING

Opening: Open with prayer and introductions. Get acquainted and register the students.

Establish Group Procedures: Determine who will lead the meetings, the time, place, and dates for the sessions.

Praise And Worship: Invite the presence of the Holy Spirit into your training session.

Distribute Manuals To Students: Introduce the manual title, format, and course objectives provided in the first few pages of the manual.

Make The First Assignment: Students will read the chapters assigned and take the Self-Tests prior to the next meeting. The number of chapters you cover per meeting will depend on chapter length, content, and the abilities of your group.

SECOND AND FOLLOWING MEETINGS

Opening: Pray. Welcome and register any new students and give them a manual. Take attendance. Have a time of praise and worship.

Review: Present a brief summary of what you studied at the last meeting.

Lesson: Discuss each section of the chapter using the **HEADINGS IN CAPITAL BOLD FACED LETTERS** as a teaching outline. Ask students for questions or comments on what they have studied. Apply the lesson to the lives and ministries of your students.

Self-Test: Review the Self-Tests students have completed. (Note: If you do not want the students to have access to the answers to the Self-Tests, you may remove the answer pages from the back of each manual.)

For Further Study: You may do these projects on a group or individual basis.

Final Examination: If your group is enrolled in this course for credit, you received a final examination with this course. Reproduce a copy for each student and administer the exam upon conclusion of this course.

MODULE: Organizing
COURSE: Biblical Management Principles

INTRODUCTION

This study presents principles of management revealed in God's written Word, the Holy Bible. "Management" is another word for "stewardship." "Stewards," or "managers," are responsible over something entrusted to them by someone else. As believers, each of us are managers of spiritual resources with which God has entrusted us.

A serious problem with many Christian leaders is that of organizing and managing these spiritual resources. If laborers for spiritual harvest are few as the Bible indicates, then they should be properly organized and mobilized.

Human growth occurs through the multiplication of living cells and the development of a skeleton to support them. For the body of Christ to grow, structure is also important. Spiritual life brings growth which we must be prepared to support.

This course is first in a series of three in the "Organizing Module" of training offered by Harvestime International Network. This study, along with the courses *"Environmental Analysis"* and *"Management By Objectives"* which follow, will help you become a good steward of spiritual resources. We recommend that these three courses be studied in order for proper understanding of the leadership, planning, and organization necessary for effective ministry.

This course introduces the subject of management, identifies leadership positions, and stresses the importance of the anointing to lead. Biblical principles of leading like a servant and shepherd and qualifications for leaders are also discussed.

Major tasks of leaders are reviewed, with emphasis on decision making and handling conflicts. Guidelines for training leaders and followers are given, and principles of success and reasons for failure examined.

The Appendix of this course provides opportunity for learning additional principles by studying examples of great leaders in the Bible.

COURSE OBJECTIVES

Upon completion of this course you will be able to:

- Define management.
- Identify spiritual resources over which believers are managers.
- Identify the main requirement for stewards.
- Identify the greatest example of spiritual leadership.
- Summarize what the ministry of management includes.
- Identify Biblical positions of leadership.
- Explain how spiritual gifts are used in ministry.
- Explain how leaders work together in ministry.
- Recognize the importance of anointing in spiritual leadership.
- List qualifications for spiritual leaders.
- Explain how to lead like a servant.
- Explain how to lead like a shepherd.
- Summarize the tasks of leaders.
- Use Biblical guidelines to make decisions.
- Use Biblical guidelines to deal with conflicts and discipline.
- Train leaders and followers.
- Turn failures into success.
- Apply Biblical principles of success.
- Identify the costs of leadership.
- Explain the true test of spiritual leadership.

CHAPTER ONE

THE MINISTRY OF MANAGEMENT

OBJECTIVES:

Upon completion of this chapter you will be able to:

- Write the Key Verse from memory.
- Define management.
- Identify spiritual resources over which believers are managers.
- Identify the main requirement for stewards.
- Identify the greatest example of leadership.
- Summarize what the ministry of management includes.

KEY VERSE:

> **To aspire to leadership is an honorable ambition. (I Timothy 3:1) New English Bible**

INTRODUCTION

This chapter introduces the ministry of management. When we speak of management we are not talking about secular management like that evident in the business world. We are speaking of managing spiritual resources for the work of the ministry.

If you learn the ministry of management, you will become a good steward of the Gospel and the ministry God has given you. You will be able to work with God to accomplish His purposes.

THE DEFINITION OF MANAGEMENT

"Management" is another word for "stewardship." "Stewards," or "managers," are responsible over something entrusted to them by someone else. Management is the process of accomplishing God's purposes and plans through proper use of human, material, and spiritual resources. Management is evaluated by whether or not these plans and purposes are accomplished. The Bible states:

> **All we like sheep have gone astray; we have turned every one to His own way... (Isaiah 53:6)**

As sheep must be directed to move along a single path, so people need direction so their efforts and energies will accomplish God's purposes and plans.

SPIRITUAL RESOURCES

All believers are stewards of certain resources given by God. These are listed in the "For Further Study" section of this lesson. In addition to these resources, leaders are stewards over special resources which include:

The Gospel: We are to share its message with others.

Finances: Every believer is a steward of their personal finances, but leaders who control money of a church or Christian organization are also stewards of these funds.

Material Resources Of Ministry: These include things such as church buildings, property, and equipment.

Spiritual Gifts: Each believer has at least one spiritual gift for which they are responsible as a steward. A leader is also responsible to help others develop their spiritual gifts.

Other Believers: If you are a leader, you are responsible for other people. You must help them mature spiritually and get involved in the work of the ministry. God uses people, not programs, to build His Kingdom. Management involves getting things done for God through people.

THE FIRST MESSAGE ON MANAGEMENT

The first message from God to man was on the subject of management. God told Adam and Eve:

> **...Be fruitful, and multiply, and replenish the earth, and subdue it...and have dominion over...every living thing that moveth upon the earth.**
> **(Genesis 1:28)**

Three important tasks of managers are contained in this verse:

1. Maximize resources by "multiplying" to accomplish God's purpose and plans.
2. Minimize disorder by "subduing."
3. Maintain order by "ruling" (dominion).

THE GREATEST EXAMPLE

The greatest example of leadership is the Lord Jesus Christ. He is the model for all Christian leaders. You will learn later in this course about the example He set by leading like a servant and a shepherd.

All the principles taught in this course are demonstrated in what Jesus did and taught. Every necessary quality of a leader was evident in the life of Christ. Every task a leader must perform was illustrated by Him. He set an example in training leaders and followers.

THE MAIN REQUIREMENT

God does not consider stewards successful because of their education, natural ability, or personality. They are successful because of their faithfulness. The main requirement of stewards is that they are faithful:

> **Moreover it is required in stewards, that a man be found faithful. (I Corinthians 4:2)**

Jesus told a parable in Matthew 25:14-30 about servants whose master gave them resources called "talents," which in this case was money. They were told to be good stewards and use the funds wisely. Those who did so were called "faithful" and were rewarded. Those who failed were judged and held accountable.

THE MINISTRY OF MANAGEMENT

The ministry of management involves leading others to accomplish great things for God. Management includes the following areas which you will study about in this course:

Recognizing The Importance Of The Anointing To Lead: Anointing by God for leadership is more important than education, talents, and experience.

Meeting Biblical Qualifications For Leadership: The management of ministry begins with the management of self.

Learning To Lead Like A Servant: Scriptural leadership is not flashy public relations and a charismatic platform personality. It is humble service to those you lead. Serving is what sets Christian leadership apart from worldly leadership.

Learning To Lead Like A Shepherd: The qualities of a shepherd in the natural world are what Jesus used to describe spiritual leadership.

Understanding The Basic Tasks Of Leaders: These include the difficult areas of decision-making and solving conflict and discipline problems.

Training Leaders And Followers: We all lead in certain situations, but everyone is a follower in other situations. Leaders must have followers. Both leaders and followers must be trained.

Applying Principles Of Success Taught In God's Word: These principles will assure successful management of spiritual resources.

Avoiding Violations That Cause Failure In Leadership: Failure in leading and following results from violations of Scriptural principles.

Understanding Principles Of Biblical Organization: These include leadership positions established by God and those developed because of practical needs of the Church.

THE BASIS OF BIBLICAL ORGANIZATION

Organization of ministry is not fixed, rigid, or based on worldly patterns. Organization is flexible to accommodate the guidance of the Holy Spirit. Management of ministry exists for the purpose of achieving God-given purposes and plans, not to create a rigid corporate, institutional structure. Organization in the Church is really more like a living organism. The Bible compares the Church to the human body, with each part working together.

You cannot be elected to leadership in God's organization. You may be elected or appointed by man to an office, but no leader is ever made by appointment or election. You must be called and equipped by God for the work of the Kingdom.

Leadership involves position, for example, positions like apostle, prophet, evangelist, pastor, and teacher. Leadership also involves function. Its main function is equipping others for the work of the ministry. Leadership also concerns the relations of leaders with their followers.

Selection and promotion as a leader comes from God:

> **For promotion cometh neither from the east, nor from the west, nor from the south.**
>
> **But God is the judge: He putteth down one, and setteth up another. (Psalms 75:6-7)**

OTHER AREAS OF MANAGEMENT

Management also involves analyzing your ministry in order to establish purpose and plans. You can learn how to conduct such a study in the Harvestime International Institute course on *"Environmental Analysis."* Management also involves the following areas about which you will learn in the Harvestime International Institute course *"Management By Objectives":*

Formulating A Purpose For Ministry In Harmony With That Of God: If you do not know your purpose and have a vision, you cannot lead others.

Making Plans To Achieve The Purpose: You will never achieve your purpose if you do not plan to do so.

Organizing People And Procedures To Implement The Plan: Management involves motivating and supervising people as they accomplish tasks which are part of God's purpose and plans.

Perfecting The Plan Through Evaluation: The Lord's work should be done with excellence.

THE IMPORTANCE OF GOOD MANAGEMENT

Here are some reasons why proper management of ministry is important:

PROVIDES PURPOSE AND DIRECTION:

If you are to be successful in ministry, then you must have a purpose and plans in harmony with those of God and be able to communicate them to others. When you know your specific purpose for ministry and make plans to fulfill that purpose, then you can lead others. Leaders must know where they are going in order to guide others. Guidance and unity in ministry involve common purpose and direction.

ELIMINATES CONFUSION:

When there is proper direction, confusion is eliminated:

> **For God is not a God of confusion but of peace. (I Corinthians 14:33)**
>
> **Therefore be imitators of God, as beloved children. (Ephesians 5:1)**

If God's activities are not characterized by confusion, the ministries of His servants should not be either.

PERMITS PROPER DECISIONS:

Decisions determine your destiny. This is true even of salvation. You make a decision to either accept or reject the Gospel and your eternal destiny is determined by your decision.

Your present life and ministry is determined by previous decisions you have made. You either made decisions by thoughtful planning or on the spur of the moment. Good management permits you to make proper decisions with the guidance of the Lord.

ESTABLISHES PRIORITIES FOR MINISTRY:

Priorities are things which are more important than other things. They are the things which take first place in your time and attention. You will have priorities in life whether you consciously determine them or not. You will establish priorities either by drifting into habits that become a

way of life, because of pressure of circumstances or people around you, or by a definite decision based on God's purposes.

PERMITS ACTION RATHER THAN REACTION:

Many ministries are occupied with reacting to urgent matters in the present instead of planning for the future. This causes leaders to react rather than act with wisdom and purpose.

Without a strategy or plan, you do not know what you are doing in ministry, why you are doing it, or how it is to be done. Because you have no organization and direction, you have nothing to commit to, no way to evaluate your effectiveness for God, and you are easily persuaded to react and quit in crisis times.

Good management transforms desire to demonstration and visions to reality. It helps you determine what you are to do and how to do it in order to fulfill God's purposes.

ESTABLISHES ACCOUNTABILITY:

In the parable of the talents in Matthew 25:14-30 the servants were accountable for all that was entrusted to their care. Their master had a plan, communicated it to them, and they were to fulfill it by investing the funds they were given.

You are accountable not only for knowing God's will for your life and ministry, but also for doing it:

> **And that servant, which knew His Lord's will, and prepared not himself, neither did according to His will, shall be beaten with many stripes. (Luke 12:47)**

If you do not wisely manage the ministry with which you are entrusted, you will be held accountable.

PERMITS EVALUATION:

Management includes evaluation to see if you are fulfilling God's purpose and plan. Understanding Biblical principles of success and reasons for failure permit such evaluation.

PERMITS WISE USE OF SPIRITUAL RESOURCES:

Good management helps you manage spiritual resources properly and enables you to be a proper steward of funds, material possessions, people, and spiritual gifts for the work of God's Kingdom.

PREPARES YOU TO ENTER OPEN DOORS:

> **For a great door and effectual is opened unto me, and there are many adversaries. (I Corinthians 16:9)**

When God opens doors, you must be ready to walk through them and face new challenges. This is not possible without proper preparation. Read the parable of the wise and foolish virgins in Matthew 25:1-13. God opens doors, but they do not stay open forever. They open and wait for you to enter. Then they close, sometimes never to open again.

HARMONIZES MINISTRY WITH GOD'S WILL:

The first question of the Apostle Paul after his conversion was, "What will you have me to do?" He was asking God, "What is your plan for my life and ministry?" Wise stewardship brings your life and ministry in harmony with God's purpose and plans.

GOD SEEKS LEADERS

God told King Saul:

> **But now thy kingdom shall not continue: the Lord hath sought him a man after his own heart, and the Lord hath commanded him to be captain over His people, because thou hast not kept that which the Lord commanded thee. (I Samuel 13:14)**

God still searches for men whom He can use as leaders:

> **And I sought for a man among them, that should make up the hedge, and stand in the gap before me for the land; that I should not destroy it; but I found none. (Ezekiel 22:30)**

> **For the eyes of the Lord run to and fro throughout the whole earth to shew himself strong in the behalf of them whose heart is perfect toward Him... (II Chronicles 16:9)**

Becoming a good manager takes time and effort:

> **Every man's work shall be made manifest: for the day shall declare it, because it shall be revealed by fire; and the fire shall try every man's work of what sort it is. (I Corinthians 3:13)**

Wood, hay, and stubble all grow above the ground. It is easily produced and can readily be seen

by man, but it is easily destroyed. Gold and silver are precious metals produced under the ground. They are not readily seen by man, but they are more lasting.
Flashy, popular, secular leadership is like the wood, hay, and stubble. It is seen of man and easily produced through natural talents and abilities. Godly leadership is like gold and silver. It is produced by the power of the Holy Spirit in the inner, hidden man. But it is infinitely precious and durable.

SELF-TEST

1. Write the Key Verse from memory.

____

____

2. Define "management."

____

3. List the spiritual resources over which believers are managers.

____

____

4. What is the main requirement for stewards?

____

5. Who is the greatest example of leadership?

____

6. Based on the discussion in this lesson, write a summary of what the "management of ministry" includes.

____

7. Why is good management important?

____

____

(Answers to tests are provided at the conclusion of the final chapter in this manual.)

FOR FURTHER STUDY

1. Jesus taught more on the stewardship of possessions than He did on Heaven, Hell, or salvation. Of the 40 parables, 19 dealt with possessions.

2. Leadership is a great responsibility because you influence others. For example, when Peter said "I go fishing," those with him immediately said, "We are going with you also." Leadership is also important because a leader is a messenger of God. See Malachi 2:7

3. Study these comparisons of worldly and spiritual management:

   -In worldly management, power is determined by skill, ability and knowledge.

   -In spiritual management, power is determined by anointing and God's authority.

   -In worldly management selection of leaders is made on the basis of factors such as skill and education.

   -In spiritual management, selection of leaders is made on the basis of anointing, calling, and revelation of God's will.

   -In worldly management, training is given in the areas of skill and knowledge.

   -In spiritual management, training should be given in a lifestyle based on God's Word into which skills must fit.

3. God cooperates with those who manage ministry. Paul said:

   Who then is Paul, and who is Apollos, but ministers by whom ye believed, even as the Lord gave to every man?

   I have planted, Apollos watered; but God gave the increase. (I Corinthians 3:5-6)

4. **Worldly management emphasizes:** / **Spiritual management emphasizes:**

Worldly management emphasizes:	Spiritual management emphasizes:
Money	Ministry
Production	Prayer
Fact	Faith
Professionalism	Anointing
Rules	Love
Skills	God's Word
Personality	Character
Intellect	Spiritual condition
Manipulation	Direction
Tasks	Relationships
Self-will	Obedience
Competition	Cooperation

5. Study this list of management responsibilities for all believers. We are responsible for:

a.	God's creation	Genesis 1:26-28
b.	Mysteries of God	I Corinthians 4:1
c.	Gospel message	I Thessalonians 2:4
d.	Spiritual gifts	I Peter 4:10
e.	Forgiveness	Matthew 6:12; 18:21-22
f.	Love	I John 4:7-8
g.	Mind	Philippians 4:8
h.	Power	Acts 1:8
i.	Time	Ephesians 5:15-16
j.	Viewpoint	I Samuel 16:7
k.	Attitude	Philippians 2:2
l.	Faith	James 2:14-17
m.	Money	II Corinthians 9:6-11
n.	Praise	Hebrews 12:15-16
o.	Ministry	Galatians 6:2
p.	Body	Romans 12:1
q.	Character	Titus 1:7-9
r.	Family	I Timothy 3:4-5, 12; 5:8

CHAPTER TWO

POSITIONS OF LEADERSHIP

OBJECTIVES:

Upon completion of this chapter you will be able to:

- Write the Key Verse from memory.
- Identify special leadership positions set in the Church by God.
- Explain how these leaders work together in ministry.
- Explain how spiritual gifts are used in leadership.
- Identify other Biblical leadership positions.

KEY VERSE:

> **And He gave some apostles; and some, prophets; and some, evangelists; and some, pastors, and teachers. (Ephesians 4:11)**

INTRODUCTION

The Church is the instrument through which God is presently working to reveal Himself to the world. In this lesson you will learn about leaders set in the Church by God. You will also learn of other leadership positions which have emerged because of practical needs in the local church.

The Bible gives specific qualifications which are to be met by those filling the leadership positions discussed in this lesson. You will study about these qualifications in Chapter Four.

SPECIAL LEADERSHIP POSITIONS

THE POSITIONS:

The Bible identifies five special leadership positions set in the Church by God:

> **And He gave some apostles; and some, prophets; and some, evangelists; and some, pastors, and teachers. (Ephesians 4:11)**

These leadership positions are established by God in the Church. They involve a special calling by God and special spiritual gifts. You should not serve in these positions just because you are asked or because you want to do so. You must be called of God and equipped with the proper spiritual gifts.

THEIR FUNCTIONS:

Here is a brief summary of the functions of these five special leadership positions:

Apostle: An apostle is one who has a special ability to develop new churches in different places and to oversee a number of churches as a supervisor. Apostle means "a delegate, one sent with full power and authority to act for another." The apostle has a special authority or ability to extend the Gospel through the world by developing organized bodies of believers. Modern terms used for an apostle are "missionary" and "church planter." The Apostle Paul is one of the best Biblical examples of an apostle.

Prophet: A prophet is one who speaks under the direct inspiration of God and holds an office of authority in the Church. A prophet has the ability to receive and communicate an immediate message of God to His people through a divinely-anointed utterance. Agabus is a good example of a New Testament prophet. See Acts 21:11

Evangelist: An evangelist has a special ability to share the Gospel with unbelievers in a way that men and women respond and become responsible members of the Body of Christ. The meaning of the word "evangelist" is "one who brings good news." Philip is a good example of an evangelist. See Acts 21:8 and chapter 8.

Pastor: The word "pastor" actually means shepherd. Pastors are leaders who assume long-term personal responsibility for the spiritual welfare of a group of believers.

Teacher: Teachers are believers who have a special ability to communicate the Word of God effectively in such a way that others learn and apply what is taught.

THEIR PURPOSE:

These special positions were established to accomplish the following purposes:

> **For the perfecting of the saints, for the work of the ministry, for the edifying of the body of Christ;**
>
> **Till we all come in the unity of the faith, and of the knowledge of the Son of God, unto a perfect man, unto the measure of the stature of the fulness of Christ.**
>
> **That we henceforth be no more children, tossed to and fro, and carried about with every wind of doctrine, by the sleight of men, and cunning craftiness, whereby they lie in wait to deceive;**
>
> **But speaking the truth in love may grow up into Him in all things which is the head, even Christ. (Ephesians 4:12-15)**

The following diagram illustrates these purposes:

God
gives

Apostles | Prophets | Evangelists | Pastors | Teachers

for

Perfecting/Equipping Of Saints

who will

Minister | Edify

resulting in

Unity | Knowledge | Perfectness

that the Body of Christ may be

No More Children (false doctrine) | Grow Up In Him (truth)

FINAL RESULT: Effective Working Of All Parts Of The Body In Love

HOW THEY WORK TOGETHER:

The five special leadership positions work together in the ministry of the Church.

The Apostle extends the Gospel to new regions to raise up new churches.

The Evangelist communicates the Gospel in such a way that unbelievers respond and are added to the Church.

The Prophet gives special messages from God to the Church by the inspiration of the Holy Spirit.

Teachers provide instruction which goes beyond the presentation of the Gospel done by the evangelist. They take new converts on to spiritual maturity and train faithful people who are capable of teaching others.

Pastors assume long-term leadership and care for the Church.

SPIRITUAL GIFTS IN LEADERSHIP

The five special leadership gifts are not the only positions of leadership in the Church. Every believer has a function in the Church:

> **But now hath God set the members, every one of them, in the body, as it hath pleased Him. (I Corinthians 12:18)**

Each believer has at least one spiritual gift. His spiritual gift equips him to fulfill his function in the Body:

> **But all these (spiritual gifts) worketh that one and the selfsame Spirit, dividing to every man severally as He will. (I Corinthians 12:11)**

We have already mentioned the special leadership gifts of apostle, prophet, evangelist, pastor, and teacher. Here is a list of the other gifts the Holy Spirit gives believers:

Speaking Gifts: Prophecy, teaching, exhortation, word of wisdom, and word of knowledge.

Serving Gifts: Serving, helps, leadership, administration, giving, showing mercy, discerning of spirits, faith, and hospitality.

Sign Gifts: Tongues, interpretation of tongues, miracles, and healings.

The Bible references which identify these gifts are:

- -Romans 12:1-8
- -I Corinthians 12:1-31
- -Ephesians 4:1-16
- -I Peter 4:7-11

(The Harvestime International Institute course, *"Ministry Of The Holy Spirit,"* discusses each of these spiritual gifts in detail. It also provides guidelines for discovering your spiritual gift.)

IMPORTANT GIFTS FOR MANAGERS

Two of these spiritual gifts, those of leadership and administration, are especially important to managers. The gift of leadership is identified in Romans 12:8 as one who "ruleth" or leads. A person with the gift of leadership has the ability to set plans in harmony with God's purpose and communicate these goals to others. He motivates others to accomplish these goals for the glory of God.

In I Corinthians 12:28, the gift of administration is called "governments." A person with this gift has the ability to give direction, organize, and make decisions on the behalf of others. The meaning of the word "governments" or "administration" is similar to that of a pilot steering a ship. A person with this gift is responsible for direction and decision-making. Like the pilot of a ship, he may not be the owner of the ship, but he has been entrusted with the responsibility of directing it on its voyage.

Titus is a Biblical example of a person with the gift of administration. The Apostle Paul started a church in Crete. Titus was the one who organized and directed it for him:

> **To Titus, mine own son...For this cause left I thee in Crete, that thou shouldest set in order the things that are wanting, and ordain elders in every city, as I had appointed thee. (Titus 1:4-5)**

The gifts of leadership and administration function well together. A person with the gift of administration has the ability to direct, organize, and make decisions. The person with the gift of leadership has the ability to motivate and work with people to achieve these goals.

EVERYONE CAN SERVE

Leadership is not limited to believers with these two gifts or the five special leadership positions. Believers with other spiritual gifts may be asked by Church leaders to serve in various leadership positions.

For example, a person with the gift of giving may be asked to lead a committee on church finance. A person with the gift of healing may be asked to lead a group of believers in ministering to the sick in local hospitals. The work of the ministry for which spiritual gifts are given involves many opportunities for leadership. Even if a believer does not have one of the leadership gifts he has the potential of becoming a leader through proper development of his own spiritual gift.

OTHER BIBLICAL POSITIONS

There are other positions of leadership mentioned in the Bible that are not spiritual gifts. They are "offices" established because of practical needs of the Church. The offices of deacon, elder, and bishop are mentioned in the New Testament. (Some people consider a bishop to be similar to a pastor. Others consider it a separate office.)

The record of the early Church was preserved by God as an example for us to follow in Church structure. These offices should also function in the Church today. The purpose of these offices is to assist those with spiritual gifts of leadership like the apostles, prophets, evangelists, pastors, teachers, and those with the gifts of leadership and administration. Use the following outline to study these positions:

Title	**References**	**Duties**
Bishop	I Timothy 3:1-7 Philippians 1:1 Titus 1:5-9 I Peter 5:2-3	Many consider a bishop to be similar to a pastor. He does have long-term care over a group of believers.
Deacon	I Timothy 3:8-13 Philippians 1:1 Acts 6:1-7	These verses indicate deacons have a ministry of serving and helps.
Deaconess	I Timothy 3:11 Romans 16:1-2	Deaconess are not specifically mentioned in the Bible. Some churches have adopted this term for the wives of deacons or other women who minister in serving or helps.
Elders	Acts 20:17,28-32 Acts 14:23; 15 Acts 16:4; 11:30 I Timothy 5:17 I Peter 5:1-4 Titus 1:5 James 5:14	These verses indicate elders provide leadership in church decisions, minister to the needs of believers, and assist in development and care of local bodies of believers.

(Note on elders: The word "elders" is first used in the Bible in Exodus 3:16 in reference to the leaders of Israel. There are many references to the elders of Israel throughout the Bible. These elders are different from the position of leadership known as an elder in the Church. The verses listed here refer to the elders in the Church rather than the elders of Israel.)

Elders, deacons, and bishops are not to run the Church independently of the special leaders (prophets, apostles, evangelists, pastors, teachers). Man selects elders, deacons, and bishops, but those with the special leadership gifts are set in the Church by God.

PRACTICAL LEADERSHIP POSITIONS

Over the years, many other leadership positions have emerged to meet both practical and organizational needs in the Church. These positions are not mentioned in the Bible, but they are important in the ministry of the local fellowship. The "For Further Study" section of this lesson lists some of these positions.

CHURCH STRUCTURE

The following diagram shows how the leadership gifts you have studied fit together in the structure of the Church:

THE CHURCH

Special Leadership Gifts:

▽

Apostles
Prophets
Evangelists
Pastors
Teachers

▽

Assisted by gifts of administration, leadership, bishops, deacons, elders, and each member of the body using their spiritual gift in the church in the place God has set them.

▽

The Foundation laid by Apostles and Prophets Ephesians 2:20

▽

BUILT UPON THE ROCK, JESUS CHRIST
Matthew 16:18 I Corinthians 3:11 Ephesians 2:20

SELF-TEST

1. Write the Key Verse from memory.

____

____

2. Look at the list of positions in List One. Read the definitions in List Two. Write the number of the definition which best describes the leadership position on the blank provided. The first one is done as an example for you.

List One	List Two
___Prophet	1. Sent with authority to act for another to develop new churches and oversee them.
___Apostle	2. Speaks under special inspiration to communicate an immediate message of God to His people; also a leadership position.
___Pastor	3. Shares the Gospel with unbelievers in a way that they respond and become responsible members of the Body of Christ; "one who brings the good news."
___Evangelist	4. Assumes long-term leadership for the spiritual welfare of believers; word means "shepherd."
___Teacher	5. Communicates God's Word in such a way that others will learn and apply what is taught; also a leadership position.
___Leadership	6. Motivates people to achieve goals.
___Administration	7. Similar to the pilot of a ship; provides direction.

3. List three other Biblical leadership offices discussed in this lesson.

_____________________ _____________________ _____________________

(Answers to tests are provided at the conclusion of the final chapter in this manual.)

FOR FURTHER STUDY

Here is a list of some other leadership positions in the local Church:

PRAYER AND HEALING MINISTRIES:

-intercessory prayer
-anointing with oil
-prayer breakfasts
-prayer groups
-hospital calls
-praying by phone
-prayer chain
-fasting
-prayer counseling

PRACTICAL MINISTRIES:

-office help
-church secretary
-preparing mailings
-church kitchen help
-nursery work
-custodial work
-repairing
-bake sales
-writing letters
-preparing Communion
-child care
-financial support
-tape ministry
-phone calling
-handling registration
-advertising
-making gifts
-sports programs
-ushering
-weddings
-making choir robes
-hospitality
-treasurer
-work groups
-recreation programs
-preparing news releases

EDUCATIONAL MINISTRIES:

-Bible teachers
-workshop leader
-youth ministry
-retreat speaker
-researching
-church library
-seminar leader
-adult classes
-children's ministries
-discipling
-Sunday school teacher
-Bible school instructor
-tutoring
-teaching new believers

COUNSELING MINISTRIES:

-prayer counseling
-marriage counseling
-teen counseling
-pregnancy counseling
-encouraging others
-home visitation
-hospital visitation
-problem solving
-follow-up calls
-crisis center
-telephone counseling

OUTREACH MINISTRIES:

-child evangelism
-bus ministry
-drama
-high school ministry
-political causes
-missions
-crusades
-TV/radio programs
-street witnessing
-college ministries
-outreach center
-coffeehouse
-men's and women's ministries
-door-to-door witness

-vacation Bible school
-Bible and literature distribution

LEADERSHIP MINISTRIES:

-organizer
-Sunday school superintendent or department superintendent
-planner
-home group leader
-missions coordinator
-leader
-committee chairman
-Christian education director
-church administrator

CARING MINISTRIES:

-hospitality
-feeding programs
-hospital visitation
-overnight guests
-clothing for needy
-nursing homes
-entertaining
-prison visitation
-helping elderly
-transportation
-baby sitting
-telephone ministry
-missions
-street ministry
-crisis center
-assisting retarded people
-assisting abused people
-helping handicapped
-helping needy
-ministry to unwed mothers

OTHER MINISTRIES:

-music
-choirs
-playing piano
-dramatic readings
-musical groups
-translation work

-drama
-leading worship
-playing organ
-puppetry
-interpreting
-bulletin boards
-writing and editing Christian material
-song writing
-church orchestra
-church band
-decorating the church for special occasions
-art

CHAPTER THREE

THE ANOINTING TO LEAD

OBJECTIVES:

Upon completion of this chapter you will be able to:

- Write the Key Verse from memory.
- Define "anointing."
- Identify three types of anointings.
- Explain the purpose of each type.
- Identify the source of spiritual anointing.
- Discuss purposes of the anointing.
- Identify the basis for the anointing of God.
- Discuss forces opposing those anointed by God.
- Explain why it is important to minister only in the position for which you are anointed.
- Explain how to maintain the fresh anointing of God.

KEY VERSE:

> **But my horn shalt thou exalt like the horn of an unicorn; I shall be anointed with fresh oil. (Psalms 92:10)**

INTRODUCTION

The Lord wants leaders to be successful and to impact the world for the Kingdom of God. How can you be that kind of leader? Having knowledge of practical areas and the general tasks of leaders will help you become a successful leader. There are Biblical qualifications for leaders which are also necessary. Spiritual gifts, skills, education, and experience are important too. You will study about these later.

But the most important thing for leaders is to be anointed by the Holy Spirit. Without the anointing of God you cannot effectively lead, organize, mobilize, or evangelize. This chapter focuses on the anointing of the Holy Spirit which is necessary for those called and chosen by God for leadership.

ANOINTING

To "anoint" means to dedicate or consecrate someone or something by applying oil. Oil is symbolic of the Holy Spirit.

THE ANOINTED ONE

The name "Christ" in the Greek language means "the anointed one." Jesus introduced His earthly ministry by proclaiming:

> **The Spirit of the Lord is upon me, because He hath anointed me... (Luke 4:18)**

Jesus made it clear that it was by the anointing of the Holy Spirit He was able to...

> **...preach the Gospel to the poor...heal the brokenhearted...preach deliverance to the captives and recovering of sight to the blind...to set at liberty them that are bruised...to preach the acceptable year of the Lord. (Luke 4:18-19)**

If it was necessary for Jesus to be anointed to minister, then it is necessary for us also.

THE THREE ANOINTINGS

There are three different anointings mentioned in the Old Testament. They are natural examples or "types" of spiritual experiences which God wants leaders to have:

THE LEPER'S ANOINTING: RELATIONSHIP

Leprosy is a dreaded disease which slowly consumes the flesh of its victim. The toes, fingers, and other body parts eventually rot and fall off.

In Old Testament times a person with leprosy was called a leper. The leper was banned from his community because the disease was contagious. To keep others from coming in contact with him he was required to cry out "unclean" wherever he went. Leprosy would slowly eat away his physical body and he would die a painful death.

In the Bible, God uses natural examples to illustrate spiritual truths. Leprosy is used as an example of sin. Just as leprosy destroys the physical body, sin will destroy you spiritually and it will destroy your ministry.

In the Old Testament law, God gave specific instructions for the cleansing of a person with leprosy. Read these in Leviticus 14 in your Bible before proceeding with this lesson. Each of the instructions you just read are symbolic of the cleansing you must experience spiritually:

A Bird Bearing Away The Guilt Of Sin: One bird slain, its blood put on the other one. This is symbolic of Jesus shedding His blood to bear away your sin.

Repentance And Confession: This is what you must do to be born again and cleansed from sin.

Running Water: This is symbolic of water baptism.

The Anointing Of Oil: This is symbolic of the work of the Holy Spirit in your life. Note that the oil was to be placed on the ear, thumb, and toe of the leper. Applying this to leadership, we must experience a similar spiritual anointing of...

The Ear: To be able to hear God's voice.

The Hand: To be able to serve Him.

The Toe: To walk in proper relationship with Him.

The most important anointing for leaders is this "leper's" anointing because it is symbolic of personal relationship. Your own relationship with God must be right if you are to lead others. You must be born-again, be able to hear God's voice, serve Him, and walk in proper relationship with Him.

THE PRIEST'S ANOINTING: HOLINESS

Leaders should also experience the priestly anointing. Read about this in Exodus 29 and 30 and in Leviticus 8 before proceeding with this lesson. The priestly anointing was an anointing for holiness, being set apart to God for His service by right living and behavior.

In Old Testament times, there were many things a priest could not do because of the holiness of his office. Because of his special anointing to lead, some things would defile a priest which might not defile other members of the congregation of Israel.

As a leader, you must experience the priestly anointing of holiness and be set apart for the service of God. You must live in harmony with God's Word. There may be things you cannot do because of the holiness of your office. Because of your special anointing to lead others, there are things which will defile you which might not defile others.

THE LEADER'S ANOINTING: POSITION AND POWER

The third type of anointing in the Old Testament is the leader's anointing. It was an anointing for those who would guide God's people as leaders, such as kings, prophets, captains, etc. The leader's anointing was one which established a leader's God-given position and gave him the power to fulfill that position.

For example, the anointing of Saul was to the position of captain over God's people:

Then Samuel took a vial of oil, and poured it upon his head, and kissed him, and said, Is it not because the Lord hath anointed thee to be captain over his inheritance? (I Samuel 10:1)

The anointing of David is recorded in I Samuel 16. This passage makes it clear that the power of the Lord came upon David because of the anointing:

So he (David's father) sent and brought him (David) in. Now he was ruddy and withal of a beautiful countenance, and goodly to look to. And the Lord said, Arise, anoint him; for this is he.

Then Samuel took the horn of oil and anointed him in the midst of his brothers; and the Spirit of the Lord came mightily upon David from that day forward. (I Samuel 16:12-13)

The leader's anointing was to impart the position, power, and authority of the office. With this anointing, God's Spirit came upon a person so he could properly lead God's people. The New Testament promise of this anointing of power is found in Acts 1:8.

But ye shall receive power, after that the Holy Ghost is come upon you: and ye shall be witnesses unto me both in Jerusalem, and in all Judaea, and in Samaria, and unto the uttermost part of the earth. (Acts 1:8)

The fulfillment of this promise is recorded in Acts 2. The Baptism in the Holy Spirit is the New Testament fulfillment of the leader's anointing of power.

The New Testament anointing of position is described in Ephesians:

And He gave some apostles; and some prophets; and some evangelists; and some, pastors, and teachers. (Ephesians 4:11)

God has anointed certain people to leadership positions in the Church and has provided the anointing of power to equip them to fulfill their callings.

THE ANOINTING IS FROM GOD

These three anointings, which are symbolic of those leaders must experience, all come from God. When Samuel anointed Saul, he said, "The Lord hath anointed thee..." (I Samuel 10:1; 15:17). When Jesus proclaimed His anointing, He said "The Lord hath anointed me" (Luke 4:18; see also Acts 10:38). It is God who raises up the anointed. God said to Samuel:

And I (God) will raise me up a faithful priest, that shall do according to that which is in mine heart and in my mind;...and he shall walk before mine anointed for ever. (I Samuel 2:35)

You do not experience the anointing by being ordained by an organization or denomination (although there is nothing wrong in doing this). The anointing for leadership comes from God:

> **But the anointing which ye have received of Him abideth in you...**
> **(I John 2:27)**

Stephen was ordained by man as a deacon. He was anointed by God as an evangelist (Acts 6). It is the anointing of God, not of man, that is most important.

THE BASIS OF THE ANOINTING

On what basis does God give this anointing? God does not anoint on the basis of intelligence, education, experience, or abilities. The anointing is not based on outward appearance. It is based on the attitude of the heart.

When Samuel went to the house of Jesse to anoint a new king, he was looking for a man with great outward appearance:

> **And it came to pass, when they were come, that he (Samuel) looked on Eliab, and said, Surely the Lord's anointed is before Him.**
>
> **But the Lord said unto Samuel, Look not on his countenance, or on the height of his stature; because I have refused him; for the Lord seeth not as man seeth; for man looketh on the outward appearance, but the Lord looketh on the heart. (I Samuel 16:6-7)**

God anointed David because of the attitude and condition of his heart. God looks at what you are inside.

PURPOSES OF THE ANOINTING

Here are some purposes of the anointing:

FULFILL GOD'S PURPOSES:

The anointing is given to leaders to enable them to fulfill God's purposes. Jesus made this quite clear:

> **The Spirit of the Lord is upon me, because He hath anointed me to preach the gospel to the poor, he hath send me to heal the brokenhearted, to preach deliverance to the captives, and recovering of sight to the blind, to set at liberty them that are bruised. (Luke 4:18)**

GIVE WISDOM TO LEAD:

The anointing gives you the wisdom to lead others instead of needing to be led:

> **But the anointing which ye have received of Him abideth in you, and ye need not that any man teach you; but as the same anointing teacheth you of all things, and is truth, and is no lie, and even as it hath taught you, ye shall abide in Him. (I John 2:27)**

DESTROY THE YOKE:

It is the anointing which destroys the spiritual yokes which bind the men and women to which you minister. The Bible indicates there are three types of yokes:

1. There is the yoke of sin:

   I am the Lord your God, which brought you forth out of the land of Egypt (sin) that ye should not be their bondsmen; and I have broken the bands of your yoke and made you go upright. (Leviticus 26:13)

2. There is the yoke which keeps people in bondage to "flesh" or "self," which is the old sin nature:

   For that which I do I allow not; for what I would, that I do not; but what I hate, that do I. (Romans 7:15)

3. There is the yoke of man which is bondage put on you by other people. This yoke can include guilt, tradition, or impossible standards of behavior which are imposed by others:
   For they bind heavy burdens and grevious to be borne and lay them on men's shoulders but they themselves will not move them with one of their fingers... (Matthew 23:4)

The anointing destroys all of these yokes:

> **...And the yoke shall be destroyed because of the anointing. (Isaiah 10:27)**

These yokes will not be destroyed by deep teaching. They will not be destroyed by education, counseling, or organization. They will be destroyed by the anointing of God upon spiritual leaders who know how to bring the message of deliverance to those in bondage.

DETERMINE POSITION:

God anoints people for specific positions or callings in ministry. For example, the position of the priests was determined "by reason of the anointing" (Numbers 18:8).

The New Testament makes it clear that God gives different spiritual gifts and callings to believers. You must know your personal calling of God, your spiritual gifts, and your specific purpose in God's plan in order to walk in the anointing of the Holy Spirit. If you try to serve in a position for which you have neither been called or anointed, you will experience difficulty. This brings us to another important point about anointing...

WALK IN YOUR OWN ANOINTING

God anoints people to specific spiritual offices, positions, and callings. Many leaders fail because they do not recognize this fact. They try to perform ministries to which they have neither been called or anointed:

> -Read Numbers 16. When Korah and his men claimed to have the same anointing as Moses, God proved differently.
>
> -Read Numbers 17. God proved His anointing rested upon Aaron in a special way.
>
> -Read I Samuel 13:8-14. When King Saul tried to serve in an office for which he had received no anointing, he was judged and rejected by God.
>
> -Read Acts 19:13-16. When the seven sons of a priest named Sceva tried to minister in an anointing they did not possess, they experienced difficulties.

Minister in your own anointing or you will be ineffective and experience great difficulties in ministry.

EXPECT OPPOSITION

If you are anointed by God you can expect opposition from Satan and his forces, as well as ungodly men:

> **The kings of the earth set themselves, and the rulers take counsel together, against the Lord, and against his anointed... (Psalms 2:2)**
>
> **Wherewith thine enemies have reproached, O Lord; wherewith they have reproached the footsteps of thine anointed. (Psalms 89:51)**

Ungodly forces want to hinder you because they know it is anointed ministry which accomplishes God's purposes.

THE FRESH ANOINTING

David speaks of "fresh oil," which is symbolic of the fresh, continued anointing of God:

> **But my horn shalt thou exalt like the horn of an unicorn; I shall be anointed with fresh oil. (Psalms 92:10)**

You maintain a fresh anointing of God's power through continually experiencing the three types of anointing previously studied.

THE LEPER'S ANOINTING: RELATIONSHIP:

Your anointing will not be fresh unless your personal relationship with God is maintained. You must keep in contact with God through prayer and Bible study if you are to hear His voice, serve Him, and walk in His ways. Ministering in position and power without relationship will result in losing your own experience and becoming a castaway:

> **But I keep under my body, and bring it into subjection: lest that by any means, when I have preached to others, I myself should be a castaway. (I Corinthians 9:27)**

> **Not every one that saith unto me, Lord, Lord, shall enter into the Kingdom of Heaven; but He that doeth the will of my Father which is in Heaven.**
>
> **Many will say to me in that day, Lord, Lord, have we not prophesied in thy name? and in thy name have cast out devils? and in thy name done many wonderful works?**
>
> **And then will I profess unto them, I never knew you; depart from me, ye that work iniquity. (Matthew 7:21-23)**

THE PRIEST'S ANOINTING: HOLINESS:

You must maintain a life of holiness if you are to experience the fresh anointing of God upon your ministry. You must be morally pure and be a person of integrity and honesty in every area of your life and ministry.

THE LEADER'S ANOINTING: POSITION AND POWER:

You must serve in the position to which God has called you. You must not emulate (imitate) the ministries and callings of others. You also must experience the continual infilling of the Holy

Spirit which assures spiritual power for the tasks God has given you.

HOW THEY FUNCTION TOGETHER

These three anointings function together to keep God's anointing fresh in your life.

-Without relationship, you cannot experience power and you will not be able to live a holy life.

-To stress holiness apart from power will result in legalism.

-To have power and position without living a holy life will put you into a situation of ministering to others while becoming a "castaway" yourself.

SELF-TEST

1. Write the Key Verse from memory.

____

____

____

2. What does it mean to "anoint"?

____

____

3. Of what is the oil symbolic?

____

____

4. List the three types of anointings discussed in this lesson and explain the meaning of each.

____

____

____

5. Who is the source of anointing for ministry?

____

6. Discuss the purposes of the anointing.

____

____

7. On what basis does God anoint? Is it because of education, experience, intelligence, etc?

____

____

____

8. Explain why ungodly forces oppose those anointed of God.

____

____

____

9. Why is it important to minister only in the position for which you are anointed by God?

____

____

____

10. How can you maintain the fresh anointing of God in your life and ministry?

____

____

____

(Answers to tests are provided at the conclusion of the final chapter in this manual.)

FOR FURTHER STUDY

1. Study about God's relationship to those who are anointed:

   -God gives deliverance and mercy to the anointed: Psalms 18:50

   -He saves and hears the anointed: Psalms 20:6

   -He looks on face of the anointed: Psalms 84:9

   -He is the saving strength of those anointed: Psalms 28:8

   -He gives revelation to those anointed (lamp of the anointed): Psalms 132:17

   -God anoints to cut off the enemy: II Chronicles 22:7

2. Study further on general facts about the anointing:

   -The first time anointing is mentioned: Genesis 31:13

   -Anointing is related to gladness and righteousness: Psalms 45:7; Hebrews 1:9

   -Natural weakness does not prevent the anointing of God: II Samuel 3:39

   -Anointing is used in the healing of the sick in Mark 6:13 and James 5:14; the blind in John 9:6;11; and the spiritually blind in Revelation 3:8.

   -Holy oil was used in Old Testament times: Exodus 30:31

   -Unity is compared to anointing: Psalms 133:2

   -Anointing is related to holiness: Exodus 29:29

   -The Word of God is anointed: Leviticus 7:36

3. You already learned how anointing was used in Old Testament times for lepers, priests, and leaders. It was also used to anoint:

   -Offerings: Exodus 29:36

   -The contents of the tabernacle: Leviticus 8, Numbers 7; Exodus 40

   -Pillars or altars: Genesis 31:13

4. Because leaders are anointed by God, we must be careful not to oppose them. See Numbers 16; I Samuel 24 and 26; II Samuel 1; I Chronicles 16:22; Psalms 105:15.

5. The anointing of man is not the same as that of God. See II Samuel 19:10. Read the tragic story of Absalom who was anointed by man (II Samuel 18-20).

6. Read about the anointing of:

-Joshua:	Deuteronomy 34:9 and Numbers 27:18,22
-Saul:	I Samuel 10:15-27
-David:	I Samuel 16:1-13
-Jesus:	Luke 4:18

7. Study Acts 7:25 and Exodus 2:11-15. Moses had the right call, but the wrong authority at first. He tried to serve in his own authority instead of God's authority.

8. Read Amos 7:14-15. Amos was not a minister. He was a herdsman and crop gatherer. But when God anointed him, he became a prophet.

CHAPTER FOUR

QUALIFICATIONS FOR LEADERS

OBJECTIVES:

Upon completion of this chapter you will be able to:

- Write the Key Verse from memory.
- Define "qualifications."
- Define the outer fruit of the Spirit.
- Define the inner fruit of the Spirit.
- Identify the two main Scriptures which list specific qualifications for leaders.
- List four qualifications required of all spiritual leaders.

KEY VERSE:

> **For we are His workmanship, created in Christ Jesus unto good works which God hath before ordained that we should walk in them.**
> **(Ephesians 2:10)**

INTRODUCTION

When God calls a believer to leadership, He wants to properly equip him to serve. Because specific tasks and callings are different, there are unique qualities necessary for various leadership positions in the Body of Christ. God equips each leader in different ways.

While God gives leaders specific qualities necessary for their own callings, there are also general qualifications which are required for all spiritual leaders. These qualifications are the subject of this lesson which discusses the basic requirements, spiritual fruit, and specific and general qualifications for leadership.

BIBLICAL QUALIFICATIONS

Qualifications are not natural abilities. They are qualities of character and conduct. Biblical qualifications for leadership are qualities of character and conduct described for leaders in God's Word. They are evidences of a godly lifestyle.

People often consider a leader's abilities as most important and ignore their qualifications for leadership. For example, people may judge a pastor on the basis of his good preaching. But while he might be able to impress people with his speaking abilities, he may be seriously lacking in the Biblical qualifications of a godly lifestyle which is required for leaders.

Spiritual leadership should be developed and evaluated on the basis of Biblical standards. The test of any ministry is not by spiritual gifts, power, or natural ability. Ministries are to be evaluated on the evidences of a godly lifestyle, also called "spiritual fruit":

> **Wherefore by their fruits you shall know them... (Matthew 7:20)**

The fruit, or spiritual qualities of a person, reveals what he is like inside:

> **For a good tree bringeth not forth corrupt fruit; neither doth a corrupt tree bring forth good fruit.**
>
> **For every tree is known by his own fruit. For of thorns men do not gather figs, nor of a bramble bush gather they grapes.**
>
> **A good man out of the good treasure of his heart bringeth forth that which is good; and an evil man out of the evil treasure of his heart bringeth forth that which is evil: for of the abundance of the heart his mouth speaketh. (Luke 6:43-45)**

A man may have personal appeal (charisma) that can be mistaken for spiritual power. He may even do miracles in the name of the Lord. But Jesus said:

> **Not every one that saith unto me, Lord, Lord, shall enter into the Kingdom of Heaven; but he that doeth the will of my Father which is in Heaven.**
>
> **In that day will they not say unto me have we not prophesied in thy name? and in thy name have cast out devils? and in thy name done many wonderful works?**
>
> **And then will I profess unto them, I never knew you: depart from me, ye that work iniquity. (Matthew 7:21-23)**

Jude warned against those who would "creep in" to the church and teach false doctrine. He said one way to recognize them was by the lack of fruit in their lives:

> **...These are...trees whose fruit withereth, without fruit, twice dead, plucked up by the roots. (Jude 12)**

The important thing in any ministry is the fruit because... "By their FRUITS ye shall know them."

THE BASICS

There are four basic requirements for all leaders. A Christian leader must be:

1. **Born Again**: He must be a true believer in Jesus Christ according to the instructions given in John 3.

2. **Baptized In The Holy Spirit**: He should have the evidence of a powerful witness as described in Acts 1:8.

3. **Called And Anointed To Be A Leader**: People must be called and anointed of God to fill leadership positions in the Church.

4. **Spiritually Mature**: A leader should not be a carnal believer (I Corinthians 3:1) or a new Christian (I Timothy 3:6). He should have experienced the foundations of faith described in Hebrews 6:1-3 and moved on to spiritual maturity as this passage directs.

Spiritual maturity involves a good personal relationship with the Lord including good prayer and Bible study habits. If you are to lead others in the ways of God, you must communicate with Him yourself and have knowledge of His Word. You can attend leadership seminars, go to college, and read many books on leadership, but unless you continue to seek the Lord your ministry will fail.

FRUIT OF THE HOLY SPIRIT

The fruit of the Holy Spirit refers to the nature of the Spirit revealed in the life of the believer. It is spiritual qualities which should be evident in the lives of all Christians, but especially in spiritual leaders.

The gifts of the Holy Spirit are for power. The fruit of the Holy Spirit is for character. Spiritual fruit is evidence of spiritual maturity. Just as fruit takes time to develop in the natural world, spiritual fruit takes time to develop. It is the product of natural growth in the life of the Spirit.

The Bible speaks of two kinds of spiritual fruit: The outer fruit of evangelism and the inner fruit of godly spiritual qualities. Spiritual leaders should bear fruit by being a powerful witness of the Gospel message:

> **Ye have not chosen me, but I have chosen you, and ordained you, that ye should go and bring forth fruit, and that your fruit should remain... (John 15:16)**

The last command of Jesus before returning to Heaven was:

Go ye into all the world and preach the Gospel to every creature. (Mark 16:15)

He challenged His disciples with a great vision of spiritual harvest:

Say not ye, There are yet four months, and then cometh harvest? behold, I say unto you, Lift up your eyes, and look on the fields; for they are white already to harvest.

And he that reapeth receiveth wages, and gathereth fruit unto life eternal: that both he that soweth and he that reapeth may rejoice together. (John 4:35-36)

Solomon said:

The fruit of the righteous is a tree of life; and he that winneth souls is wise. (Proverbs 11:30)

The power of the Holy Spirit enables believers to be spiritually fruitful through evangelism:

But ye shall receive power after that the Holy Ghost is come upon you: and ye shall be witnesses unto me both in Jerusalem, and in all Judaea, and in Samaria, and unto the uttermost part of the earth. (Acts 1:8)

The method of spiritual reproduction is given in II Timothy 2:2:

And the thing that thou hast heard of me among many witnesses, the same commit thou to faithful men, who shall be able to teach others also. (II Timothy 2:2)

Because of the importance of the fruit of evangelism, Harvestime International Institute offers a course on this subject entitled *"Leaven-Like Evangelism."*

In addition to the spiritual fruit of evangelism, leaders should also develop the fruit of Christ-likeness:

But the fruit of the Spirit is love, joy, peace, longsuffering, gentleness, goodness faith,

Meekness, temperance: against such there is no law. (Galatians 5:22-23)

These are inner qualities the Holy Spirit wants to develop in the life of a leader. They are qualities that were evident in the life of Jesus Christ. This is why we call them "Christ-like qualities."

The fruit of the Holy Spirit is found in every act of goodness, righteousness, and truth done by believers:

> **For the fruit of the Spirit is in all goodness and righteousness and truth. (Ephesians 5:9)**

The fruit of the Holy Spirit also includes the following specific qualities:

LOVE:

Love is an emotion of deep affection, care, and concern. It involves caring for people, being friendly, sympathetic, compassionate, understanding, comforting, encouraging, and attentive.

The leader must love God (Mark 12:30). Love is to be shown by the leader to his followers, all believers, and the unsaved (I Peter 1:22; Luke 6:27,32,35; Matthew 5:43-44; 19:19; John 13:34-35; 15:9,12; 17:26; I John 2:9-10).

The leader's work for the Lord is to be a labor of love (I Thessalonians 1:3). Faith works by love (Galatians 5:6) and spiritual gifts work through love (I Corinthians 13). Love is the key to success of all ministry (I Corinthians 13).

Love involves tact, which is an ability to get along with others and relate to them in a positive manner. It is an ability to say and do what is necessary and difficult without offending others.

JOY:

Joy is a quality of gladness, delight, and jubilance. It is God's desire that you have joy (John 15:11; 17:13). The disciples were filled with joy and the Holy Ghost (Acts 13:52). The source of joy is not in worldly things. It is in God (Psalms 16:11). Because true joy is spiritual and not dependent on outward circumstances, the leader can rejoice in temptation and trials (James 1:2; II Corinthians 7:4). He can be longsuffering with joy (Colossians 1:11).

PEACE:

Peace is a condition of quiet, calm, tranquility, and harmony. It is the absence of strife, anxiety, and concern. A leader with this quality is reliable and able to keep his head in emergencies because he can keep calm.

Confusion is the opposite of peace. God does not cause confusion. His desire is to bring peace (I Corinthians 14:33). All true peace comes through Jesus Christ (Acts 10:36; Ephesians 2:14; Romans 5:1; John 14:27; 16:33).

Leaders should follow after things which result in peace (Romans 14:19) and live in peace with others (II Corinthians 13:11; Hebrews 12:14). Unity, which is necessary in any effective ministry, is kept through peace (Ephesians 4:3). The peace of God must rule the heart of the ruler (Colossians 3:15).

LONGSUFFERING:

Longsuffering is the quality of patience. It is the ability to cheerfully bear an unbearable situation and patiently endure. Longsuffering was a quality evident in the ministry of the Apostle Paul (II Timothy 3:10). We are to be longsuffering with joyfulness (Colossians 1:11).

The leader should preach God's Word with longsuffering (II Timothy 4:2) and relate to others with this quality (Ephesians 4:2). He must "put on" longsuffering as a spiritual quality (Colossians 3:12).

GENTLENESS:

Gentleness is the quality of having a mild manner, not being severe, violent, or loud. It is a quiet and respectful kindness. The Bible warns believers not to strive but to be gentle to all men (II Timothy 2:24). We are not to be brawlers. Brawlers are people who are always fighting or arguing (Titus 3:2). We are to be easily entreated. That means we are to be easily approached by others because of our gentle nature (James 3:17).

A gentle leader is a great leader. David wrote:

> **Thou hast also given me the shield of thy salvation; and thy right hand hath holden me up, and thy gentleness hath made me great. (Psalms 18:35)**

GOODNESS:

Goodness is acts of holiness or righteous acts. God fills the hungry with goodness (Psalms 107:9). As believers, the goodness and mercy of God follow us (Psalms 23:6).

FAITH:

Faith is an attitude of belief, expectation, and hope towards God (Hebrews 12:1). It is believing that all God said is true and that nothing is impossible. Faith, combined with the work of the ministry, accomplishes great things for the Kingdom of God.

Faith is an attitude of confidence in God which makes followers feel confident and builds their faith. It is the belief that "I can do all things through Christ which strengtheneth me."

MEEKNESS:

Meekness is controlled strength. Disciplining of others should be done in meekness (Galatians 6:1) and it helps the leader keep unity in the church (Ephesians 4:1-3). It should be used in dealing with all men (Titus 3:2; II Timothy 2:24-25). A wise man is a meek man (James 3:13). All believers are encouraged to seek this quality (Colossians 3:12; I Timothy 6:11; Zephaniah 2:3).

TEMPERANCE:

Temperance is moderation in emotions, thought, and actions. It is self-control. Temperance is mastery in all things (I Corinthians 9:27 and 9:19- 27). We are to add temperance to our lives (II Peter 1:6).

SPECIFIC QUALIFICATIONS

In addition to spiritual fruit, the Bible identifies specific qualifications for leaders. These are found in I Timothy 3 and Titus 1. The following qualifications are those listed for pastors, bishops, elders, or deacons. Although these qualifications are identified for specific offices, they are desirable for all leadership positions:

BISHOPS AND ELDERS:

Above Reproach: Should have a good reputation, moral, disciplined, and not be in violation of God's Word: I Timothy 3:2; Titus 1:6,7

Husband Of One Wife: If married, should have only one mate: I Timothy 3:2; Titus 1:6. (The support and cooperation of the mate in ministry is also important.)

Temperate: Moderate in all things: Titus 1:8; I Timothy 3:2

Self-controlled: Demonstrate control in all areas of life and conduct. If a man is to lead others, he must be able to control himself: Titus 1:8

Sober, Vigilant: This means the leader is knowledgeable, sensible, wise, and practical: I Timothy 3:2; Titus 1:8

Hospitable: Home is open to others: I Timothy 3:2; Titus 1:8

Able To Teach: Has an ability to communicate God's Word to others: I Timothy 3:2; Titus 1:9

Not Addicted To Wine: I Timothy 3:3; Titus 1:7

Patient: Opposite of being quick tempered: I Timothy 3:3

Not Self-willed: Not self-centered and always wanting their own way: Titus 1:7

Not A New Convert: Must have maturity and experience as a believer: I Timothy 3:6

Loving What Is Good: Supporting all that is worthwhile to God and His purposes: Titus 1:8

Just: Fair in dealing with people: Titus 1:8

Stable In The Word: Titus 1:9

Holy: Righteous, sanctified: Titus 1:8

Not Fond Of Sordid Gain: Not greedy for financial gain. Free from the love of money: Titus 1:7; I Timothy 3:3

Manages His Own Household Well: Must show leadership ability in his own family: I Timothy 3:4-5

Having Children Who Believe: Must have children who have responded to the Lord and are not rebellious: Titus 1:6

Good Reputation With Those Outside: Must have a good testimony among non-believers: I Timothy 3:7

DEACONS:

Dignity: Must be respected and demonstrate a serious mind and character: I Timothy 3:8

Not Double Tongued: Does not give conflicting reports: I Timothy 3:8

Not Addicted To Much Wine: I Timothy 3:8

Not Fond Of Sordid Gain: Not greedy for financial gain: I Timothy 3:8

Settled In His Commitment To The Faith: I Timothy 3:9

Tested: A person who has undergone spiritual trials and temptations and proven faithful: I Timothy 3:10

Beyond Reproach: The absence of any charge of bad conduct: I Timothy 3:10

Husband Of One Wife: If married, should have one mate: I Timothy 3:12

Good Managers Of Household: Must demonstrate leadership in family life: I Timothy 3:12

Proven: Not a new convert, but proven as a believer: I Timothy 3:10

GENERAL QUALIFICATIONS

Here are some additional qualifications which are important for leaders:

VISION:

A man who leads must have vision. Vision involves knowing your purpose in God's plan, being able to hear God's voice, and knowing His will and purposes.

Paul was a good example of a leader with vision. Paul was able to lead others because he had a clear vision of what God had called him to do. In the later years of his ministry he said, "I was not disobedient to the heavenly vision."

Vision enables a leader to project into the future beyond the present and believe God for great things.

EXCELLENCE:

A leader should show concern for excellence, not settling for "average" or "good enough" in the work of the Lord. He should be efficient and competent, not slothful in ministry. He should be punctual, thorough, loyal, and dependable.

DECISIVENESS:

"Decisiveness" means the ability to make firm decisions, not being swayed back and forth in indecision. When all the facts are in, the ability to make a swift and clear decision is the mark of a good leader.

HUMOR:

A good sense of humor, which is the ability to see the funny side of things, will help in difficult situations.

COURAGE:

A leader must not be fearful. He must be courageous and able to stand in the face of opposition by Satan or man (Nehemiah 6:11).

A POSITIVE ATTITUDE:

Discouragement and a negative attitude result in defeat. Difficult circumstances are tests to leadership. Do they discourage you? Do they destroy, defeat, or deter you? Leaders must develop a positive attitude, a spirit of encouragement instead of discouragement. Your attitude will not only affect your performance as a leader, but will be communicated to your followers. A negative, discouraged leader has negative, discouraged followers.

EQUIPPER:

The main task of leadership is to equip people for the work of the ministry (Ephesians 4:12). An equipper is able to organize, motivate, and mobilize people. He shows zeal and enthusiasm for the work of God. He communicates these attitudes to followers and motivates and encourages them for the work of the ministry.

As part of equipping, he knows how to delegate tasks to others instead of doing everything himself. A good leader builds other leaders. An equipper is strong enough to allow others to have a ministry, responsibility, authority, and praise without feeling threatened.

AUTHORITY:

A leader should be a man of authority under the authority of God. He must be able to lead with the power and authority delegated to him by God.

DEDICATED:

A leader should be committed and dedicated to God, His Kingdom, those he leads, and the work of the ministry.

INITIATOR:

Some leaders are *imitators*. They copy what others do.

Some leaders are *maintainers*. They simply maintain what has already been started. They are bound in tradition.

Some leaders are *conformers*. They conform to the will of the people and the claim that "we have always done it this way."

Good leaders are *initiators*. They are flexible and open to change. They are not rigid and bound in tradition. This type of leader is creative and original, open to be inspired by the Holy Spirit to new ways of doing things and new ideas. They are able to adjust priorities, change methods, and do "whatever," "whenever" necessary for the advancement of the Kingdom.

WISDOM AND KNOWLEDGE:

The leader should evidence sound thinking and wisdom in decisions and actions. He must have adequate mental ability to know how to lead. These skills can be gained through training, experience, and guidance of the Holy Spirit.

EDUCATION:

Education is important, but remember that Jesus chose ignorant and unlearned men. They became great leaders because of the power of God.

EXPERIENCE:

Because Joshua was a man with warfare experience, he was selected to lead Israel into the promised land. This is why "Body ministry" by every believer is important. It provides experience that raises up new leaders.

WILLING TO PAY THE COST:

Jesus said there was a cost to true discipleship. He cautioned potential disciples to count the cost. Leaders must be willing to take up the cross, deny themselves, and work hard under difficult, lonely circumstances.

A SERVING SPIRIT:

Jesus indicated that the qualifications of leaders in God's Kingdom differed from those of worldly leaders. Christian leaders must develop a humble, compassionate, serving spirit and lead like a shepherd. These qualifications are so important that the next two lessons focus on them.

DEVELOPING QUALITIES

As you study the lists of spiritual fruit, specific, and general qualifications discussed in this lesson, you may be overwhelmed at the qualities necessary for leadership. You may think, "I can never develop all of these qualities!"

...And you are right. There is no such thing as a "self-made" leader. In other words, you cannot develop these qualities in yourself by yourself. The qualifications of a leader can only be developed by allowing the power of the Holy Spirit to work in your life.

The process is a continuous one, for the Bible indicates we "are" His workmanship. The word "are" is in present tense and means we are constantly under development through the creative power of God:

For we are His workmanship, created in Christ Jesus unto good works which God hath before ordained that we should walk in them.
(Ephesians 2:10)

SELF-TEST

1. Write the Key Verse from memory.

____

____

____

2. What does the word "qualifications" mean?

____

3. What is the fruit of evangelism?

____

4. What is the fruit of Christ-like qualities?

____

5. Look at the fruit of the Holy Spirit in List One. Read the definitions in List Two. Write the number of the definition which best describes the fruit on the blank provided.

List One	**List Two**
_____Temperance	1. Deep affection, care
_____Faith	2. Gladness, delight
_____Meekness	3. Quiet, calm, harmony
_____Gentleness	4. Patient endurance
_____Goodness	5. Mild manner, not severe
_____Joy	6. Righteous acts
_____Longsuffering	7. Strong confidence in God
_____Peace	8. Controlled strength
_____Love	9. Self-control

6. Identify the two main Bible references which give specific qualifications for leaders in the Church:

____

____

7. What are four basic qualifications required of all leaders?

____

____

____

____

(Answers to tests are provided at the conclusion of the final chapter in this manual.)

FOR FURTHER STUDY

1. Jesus Christ had all the fruit of the Holy Spirit evident in His life. Study the following examples.

   Outer Fruit:

-Evangelism:	John 10:16; Mark 1:38

   Inner Fruit:

-Love:	Mark 10:21; John 11:5,36
-Joy:	John 15:11
-Peace:	John 14:27
-Longsuffering:	I Peter 3:15
-Gentleness:	II Corinthians 10:1
-Goodness:	Romans 11:22
-Faith:	Matthew 17:14-21
-Meekness:	II Corinthians 10:1
-Temperance:	Luke 4:1-13

2. Study again the specific and general qualifications for leaders discussed in this lesson. Find Scripture references in the Gospels which illustrate these qualities in the life and ministry of Jesus.

3. Review the lists of qualifications given for leaders in this lesson. Evaluate your own life. How do you measure up to each of these?

4. Read the story of Jesus cursing the fig tree in Matthew 21:18-20. Jesus did not curse the fig tree just because he was angry that the tree had no fruit. He was teaching an important truth. The fig tree had a good appearance. It had green leaves and looked as if it should be fruitful, but it had no fruit.

   It is not enough to have the appearance of spirituality. Some leaders give the outward appearance of having everything under control, but inwardly they do not have the spiritual fruit of Christ-likeness. This was the condition of the Pharisees, a religious group of leaders at the time of Christ. Jesus said to them:

   Woe unto you, scribes and Pharisees, hypocrites! for ye are like unto whited sepulchers, which indeed appear beautiful outward, but are within full of dead men's bones, and of all uncleanness. (Matthew 23:27)

In leaders, as well as all believers, God is concerned about fruitfulness rather than the appearance of fruitfulness.

5. Note the five qualifications that Moses stipulated for the future leader of Israel (Numbers 27:17). He was to be a man who:

   1. May go out before them: One who would lead.
   2. May go in before them: A person who could intercede in behalf of the people.
   3. Could lead them out: One who would be an able leader in warfare.
   4. Who would bring them in: A person able to lead them into the land.
   5. Would give proper leadership so that "the congregation of the Lord be not as sheep which have no shepherd."

6. Here are some contrasts between worldly and spiritual leaders:

The Worldly Leader	**The Spiritual Leader**
Self-confident	Confident in God
Knows men	Also knows God
Makes his own decisions	Seeks God's will
Ambitious	Humble
Follows his own methods	Follows God's methods
Enjoys obedience from others	Obeys God
Motivated by personal desires	Motivated by love
Independent	God-dependent

7. Proverbs 28 contrasts qualifications of a good leader with those of a wicked leader:

A Good Leader:

-Is stable (does not flee, is bold): Verses 1-2
-Stands for what is right despite conflicts: Verse 4
-Keeps the law: Verses 4, 9
-Understands all things by seeking the Lord for revelation knowledge: Verses 5, 11
-Makes his parents proud: Verse 7
-Is honest: Verses 6, 8
-Is a man of prayer: Verse 9
-Is prosperous (all good things): Verses 10, 20, 25
-Is a man of discernment (searcheth out understanding): Verse 11
-Brings joy: Verse 12
-Confesses his sins: Verse 13
-Fears God: Verse 14

-Is not covetous: Verse 16
-Will rule a long time: Verse 16
-Is peaceful: Verse 17
-Walks uprightly: Verse 18
-Is diligent: Verse 19
-Is faithful: Verse 20
-Is not a respecter of persons: Verse 21
-Is not afraid of confrontation and discipline: Verse 23
-Makes his family a priority: Verse 24
-Is humble and trusts in the Lord instead of himself: Verse 25
-Trusts in God's guidance: Verse 26
-Is compassionate and considerate of those around him: Verse 27
-Causes righteous men to increase: Verse 28

A Wicked Leader:

-Is fearful and flees when there is no need: Verse 1
-Is unstable: Verses 1-2
-Oppresses the poor: Verse 3
-Is proud and swayed by man's praise; he is popular with the unrighteous: Verse 4
-Has no depth (he is more like sweeping rain): Verse 3
-Lacks compassion: Verses 3, 27
-Forsakes the law: Verse 4
-Lacks understanding: Verses 5, 16
-Is perverse in his ways: Verses 6, 18
-Is a companion of riotous (unruly) men: Verse 7
-Makes his parents ashamed: Verse 7
-Increases unjustly: Verse 8, 20, 22
-Does not pray: Verse 9
-Causes the righteous to go astray: Verse 10
-Is wise in his own conceit: Verse 11
-His rise to power bring fear: Verses 12, 28
-Covers his sins: Verse 13
-Hardens his heart: Verse 14
-Rules like a roaring lion or angry bear: Verse 15
-Is violent: Verses 15, 17
-Is covetous: Verse 16
-Is destined to fall: Verses 10, 18
-Falls into mischief: Verse 14
-Follows after vanity (is lazy, influenced by great people): Verse 19
-Takes bribes, has respect of persons: Verse 21
-Is guilty: Verse 20
-Lives in spiritual poverty: Verse 22
-Is a flatterer (insincere in compliments): Verse 23

-Does not make his family a priority: Verse 24
-Is proud: Verse 25
-Stirs up strife: Verse 25
-Trusts in his own abilities to direct him: Verse 26
-Destroys instead of builds: Verse 24
-Is inconsiderate of those around him: Verse 27

Summary Of These Contrasts: See Verse 28

CHAPTER FIVE

LEADING LIKE A SERVANT

OBJECTIVES:

Upon completion of this chapter you will be able to:

- Write the Key Verses from memory.
- Identify one leadership style that is uniquely Christian.
- Identify the greatest example of servant leadership.
- Explain how leading like a servant results in power.
- List four contrasts between secular and Christian leaders.
- Identify who we serve.
- Explain how to become a servant leader.

KEY VERSES:

> **Let this mind be in you, which was also in Christ Jesus;**
>
> **Who, being in the form of God, thought it not robbery to be equal with God;**
>
> **But made Himself of no reputation, and took upon Him the form of a servant, and was made in the likeness of men. (Philippians 2:5-7)**

INTRODUCTION

Leadership in the world is often measured by power, money, education, and abilities. There are many styles of leadership in the world. By "style" we mean the way in which a person leads. For example, there are dictators who control people. There are also democratic leaders who are controlled by the vote of the people.

When Jesus came into the world, He reversed the world's concept of successful leadership when He became a servant. This chapter concerns the New Testament principle of leading like a servant.

A CONTRASTING EXAMPLE

Jesus contrasted spiritual leadership with worldly leadership. He said:

...Ye know that they which are accounted to rule over the Gentiles exercise lordship over them; and their great ones exercise authority upon them.

But so shall it not be among you: but whosoever will be great among you, shall be your minister:

And whosoever of you will be the chiefest, shall be servant of all. (Mark 10:42-44)

Leading like a servant is what sets Christian leadership apart from worldly leadership. It is the one leadership style that is uniquely Christian.

THE GREATEST EXAMPLE

The greatest example of leading like a servant was the Lord Jesus Christ. A servant is one who serves others in humbleness, dedication, and love. Jesus both taught and modeled servanthood. Jesus rejected all the ideas of power held in the world and proposed something new. "Servant" is a strange word for a leader, but Jesus made it clear He had come to serve:

...But I am among you as he that serveth. (Luke 22:26)

Mark relates that Jesus came not to be served, but to serve:

For even the Son of man came not to be ministered unto, but to minister, and to give his life a ransom for many. (Mark 10:45)

Paul said that Jesus...

...made Himself of no reputation, and took upon Him the form of a servant, and was made in the likeness of men. (Philippians 2:7)

FOLLOWING THE PATTERN

The leaders in the early Church followed the pattern set by Jesus. They called themselves servants:

Paul, a servant of Jesus Christ... (Romans 1:1)
James, a servant of God and...Christ. (James 1:1)
Peter, a servant...of Jesus Christ. (II Peter 1:1)
Jude, a servant of...Jesus Christ. (Jude 1:1)
Grant to thy servants to speak thy Word with all boldness. (Acts 4:29)

We are to continue in this pattern. We are to be servants of those whom we lead.

THE POWER OF THE SERVANT

You may ask, "How can I be a leader if I am a servant to the people I am leading? Why all this emphasis on serving?" The answer to these questions is that in servanthood there is power. Leading like a servant does not mean being a weak leader. It is not to say that leadership should not be energetic, aggressive, and strong against spiritual enemies.

The power of servanthood is that it humbles a person to the point that he can be used by God. This is illustrated in the life of Jesus Christ. Read Philippians 2:5-11 in your Bible. (You will study this passage in detail later in this lesson). These verses explain how through humbling Himself as a servant and dying on the cross (verses 5-8), Jesus was exalted in great power (verses 9-11). The cross was the last place on earth anyone would look for a leader, but it became the "power of God unto salvation" (I Corinthians 1:18). In God's Kingdom, the order of many things is reversed. We are strong when we are weak, receive when we give, and live by dying. As a leader, you become powerful through serving.

FOUR CONTRASTS

Read Matthew 20:25-28 and Mark 10:42-44. These passages show four qualities of worldly leaders that contrast the characteristics of Christian leaders:

1. Secular leaders have *dominion* over their followers: "Dominion" in this text means "oppressive, controlling force." Servant leaders do not oppress or control their followers.

2. Secular leaders exercise *authority* over followers: The word "authority" in this text means "superiority." Worldly leaders consider themselves superior to their followers. Christian leaders are called to service, not superiority.

3. Secular leaders are *chiefs* over their followers: The word "chief" in this text means to be in first place. In God's Kingdom, the first (leaders) are last.

4. Secular leaders are *lords* over those they lead: The word "lord" means one to whom service is due. The Christian leader serves his followers.

WHO DO WE SERVE?

As servant leaders, we serve the Body of Christ. Paul told the Corinthians:

> **For we preach not ourselves, but Christ Jesus the Lord; and ourselves your servants for Jesus' sake. (II Corinthians 4:5)**

We also serve lost and dying humanity. Read the parable of the good Samaritan in Luke 10:25-37. Servanthood takes on dignity and power because when we serve others, we are really serving the Lord:

And the King shall answer and say unto them, Verily I say unto you, Inasmuch as ye have done it unto one of the least of these my brethren, ye have done it unto me. (Matthew 25:40)

Read the parable of the servants in Matthew 25:14-30. Because we are serving the Lord, we are responsible to Him:

Verily, verily, I say unto you, The servant is not greater than His lord, neither he that is sent greater than he that sent him. (John 13:16)

HOW TO BECOME A SERVANT LEADER

Read Philippians 2:5-8. This passage explains how to become a servant leader by following the example of Christ. Leading like a servant means you must:

DEVELOP THE PROPER ATTITUDE:

Leading like a servant begins with your attitude. You must develop the attitude of Jesus:

Let this mind be in you, which was also in Christ Jesus;

Who, being in the form of God, thought it not robbery to be equal with God...and took upon Him the form of a servant. (Philippians 2:5-7)

God uses men and women whose heart attitude is right. David was anointed as king because the Lord looked at his heart (I Samuel 16:7). Motives are determined in the heart. Our natural motives are selfish. If you are to be a servant leader, your attitudes and motives must change.

HUMBLE YOURSELF:

But made Himself of no reputation, and took upon Him the form of a servant... (Philippians 2:7)

Do not be concerned about your ambitions, plans, position, or reputation. Yield all of these

things to God and humble yourself. Humbling yourself is something you do, not something God does.

IDENTIFY WITH MANKIND:

Jesus was able to serve because he identified Himself with mankind. He identified and met their needs:

...and was made in the likeness of men...and being found in fashion as a man... (Philippians 2:7-8)

Jesus was tempted like man, suffered like man, and had a body subject to the weaknesses and needs of mortal man. If you are to serve those you lead, you must identify yourself with them in their weaknesses, sufferings, and needs.

BE OBEDIENT:

In order to serve, Jesus became obedient:

...He...became obedient... (Philippians 2:8)

Everyone who is in authority as a leader is also under the authority of a leader. As a Christian leader, you are under the authority of God. You may also be under a leader of a denomination or Church fellowship. To properly serve as a leader, you must be obedient to your own leaders.

DIE TO SIN AND SELF:

Jesus was obedient event to the point of death:

...and became obedient unto death, even the death of the cross. (Philippians 2:8)

Paul said "I die daily" (I Corinthians 15:31). The dying of which he spoke was a continuous dying to sin and self. This is what is required of those who would lead by serving. You must crucify sin and self in your life. The cross will be a painful experience, but as Jesus, you will learn the principles of servant leadership through the suffering.

SERVE IN LOVE:

Because of His great love, Jesus humbled Himself, took the form of a servant, identified with man and became obedient unto death:

Herein is love, not that we loved God, but that He loved us, and sent His Son to be the propitiation for our sins.

Beloved, if God so loved us, we ought also to love one another. (I John 4:10-11)

Love is central to servant leadership. Love begins as an emotion in the heart, but it is shown in practical, observable ways. When you truly love someone, you are willing to serve them.

A servant leader builds up those he serves. He never uses people but works with and through them in a way that helps them grow spiritually. He gives instead of takes. Destruction is fast and easy but building takes time and is more difficult.

Read I Corinthians 13. Each place it says "charity" substitute the words "the servant leader." (Example: "the servant leader suffereth long.") This will help you grasp the meaning of the love that is to be shown by servant leaders.

LET GOD BE IN CHARGE:

When Jesus came to earth as a servant, He gave up His right to "be in charge" of His own life. He said, "Not my will, but thine be done." When you choose to be a servant, you give up the right to be in charge. You are no longer building your own kingdom. You are building God's Kingdom. You no longer communicate your ideas or beliefs. You communicate the message of your Master. It is no longer your will, but God's will. Jesus came to serve by choice. Now the choice is yours...Will you choose to serve? Remember: You are only qualified to lead to the degree you are willing to serve.

SELF-TEST

1. Write the Key Verses from memory.

____

____

2. What is the one leadership style that is uniquely Christian?

____

3. Who is the greatest example of servant leadership?

____

4. Explain how leading like a servant results in power.

____

5. List four contrasts between secular and Christian leaders.

_______________ _______________

_______________ _______________

6. As leaders, who do we serve?

____

7. Using Philippians 2:5-8, explain how to become a servant leader.

____

____

____

(Answers to tests are provided at the conclusion of the final chapter in this manual.)

FOR FURTHER STUDY

Read this verse:

> **For he that in these things serveth Christ is acceptable to God and approved of men. (Romans 14:18)**

This verse identifies the results of successful leadership:

1. Serving Christ, which results in...
2. Being acceptable to God and...
3. Being approved by man.

Now study Romans chapters 12-14. Make a list of the things which you are to do in order to be a servant of Christ, acceptable to God and approved of men. Here is an example to follow:

Reference	**What I Must Do**
Romans 12:1	Present my body as a living sacrifice, holy and acceptable to God.
__________	______________________________
__________	______________________________
__________	______________________________
__________	______________________________
__________	______________________________
__________	______________________________
__________	______________________________
__________	______________________________
__________	______________________________
__________	______________________________
__________	______________________________

CHAPTER SIX

LEADING LIKE A SHEPHERD

OBJECTIVES:

Upon completion of this chapter you will be able to:

- Write the Key Verse from memory.
- Identify the Good Shepherd.
- Identify the one true sheepfold.
- Summarize responsibilities of the shepherd.
- Summarize warnings to bad shepherds.
- Apply natural principles of shepherding to leadership.

KEY VERSES:

> **Feed the flock of God which is among you, taking the oversight thereof, not by constraint, but willingly; not for filthy lucre, but of a ready mind;**
>
> **Neither as being lords over God's heritage, but being ensamples to the flock. (I Peter 5:2-3)**

INTRODUCTION

Another analogy or natural parallel illustrating leadership is that of a shepherd. In the natural world, a shepherd is one who cares for sheep. A "fold" is a group or flock of sheep. In the spiritual world, people are compared to sheep. We are either sheep who have gone astray spiritually (Isaiah 53:6) or who have become part of the "fold" or "flock" of the Lord.

Jesus referred to Himself as the "Good Shepherd" and explained in detail what shepherding involves. This example is one of the greatest illustrations of spiritual leadership (see John 10). To be an effective leader, you must not only know the Good Shepherd and be related to Him personally, you must also learn how to lead like a shepherd.

Peter confirms that we are to lead like shepherds:

> **Feed the flock of God which is among you, taking the oversight thereof... (I Peter 5:2)**

PRINCIPLES OF SHEPHERDING

Since Jesus called Himself the "Good Shepherd," then we must study His example of ministry to understand principles of shepherding. Turn to John 10 in your Bible and use it to guide you as you study these basic principles of shepherding:

ONE FOLD, ONE SHEPHERD:

The first principle that must be understood is that there is only one fold and one shepherd. The "fold" is the Church which is composed of all born again believers. The "shepherd" is Jesus Christ. There is only one way into the fold, and that is through Jesus:

> **I am the door; by me if any man enter in, he shall be saved, and shall go in and out, and find pasture. (John 10:9)**
>
> **...and there shall be one fold, and one shepherd. (John 10:16)**

In the natural world, human shepherds divide their flocks from other flocks because it is easier and more practical to care for them. They can only be responsible and care for so many. This is true also in spiritual leadership. But in reality, there is only one fold. It is made up of all true believers who belong to the Good Shepherd, Jesus Christ. As a leader or "shepherd," you are actually an "under-shepherd." You serve over part of His flock "under" the direction of the Good Shepherd.

Always remember that divisions of denomination, organization, and local church fellowships are made by man and exist only to permit personal care and practical organization. In reality, there is only one fold.

Do not try to separate "your flock" from other people in the flock of the Good Shepherd by denominationalism. Do not be concerned with building "your flock" of denomination or the local fellowship. Be concerned with building the flock of the Good Shepherd. Do not set rules and regulations of man to exclude some sheep. Jesus declares, "Whosoever will may come," as long as they come through the door of the Lord Jesus Christ.

God's fold is not exclusive. The door is open to all of His sheep:

> **And other sheep, I have, which are not of this fold: them also I must bring, and they shall hear my voice, and there shall be one fold, and one shepherd. (John 10:16)**

SHEEP ARE GIVEN BY GOD:

Because there is only one fold, all sheep (followers) are given by God:

My Father, which gave them (the sheep) me, is greater than all... (John 10:29)

Followers are only entrusted to your care. In reality, they belong to God.

SOME SHEEP WILL NOT FOLLOW:

There is a sad fact of which you must be aware as a shepherd. Some who are called will refuse to follow. Jesus said:

But ye believe not, because ye are not of my sheep... (John 10:26)

There will be some who are called but will not follow. They will refuse to become part of the fold. It is a sad fact, but true. Do not let this discourage you. Lead those who will follow.

THE SHEPHERD KNOWS HIS SHEEP:

Jesus said:

I am the good shepherd and know my sheep, and am known of mine. (John 10:14)

In the time of Christ's ministry, shepherds had a very personal relationship with their sheep. The shepherd was there at the birth of the sheep and he guided and cared for it throughout its lifetime. To be an effective leader, you must know the people entrusted to your care. You must develop a personal relationship with them. Jesus said the Good Shepherd "calleth His own sheep by name" (John 10:3).

THE SHEEP KNOW THE SHEPHERD:

Not only does the shepherd know his sheep, the sheep know the shepherd:

My sheep hear my voice, and I know them, and they follow me. (John 10:27)

Jesus said that the sheep know the voice of the shepherd. They listen and follow because they know and trust him.

As a leader, you must build relationships of love and trust with your followers. To do this, you must be with your sheep and be available to them, not separated from them. You must conduct your own life so that the sheep can follow you as you follow Christ:

Be ye followers of me, even as I also am of Christ. (I Corinthians 11:1)

People do not follow you merely because you are assigned as a leader. You must gain their trust in order to lead them. You do this by letting them get to know you.

THE SHEPHERD CARES FOR THE SHEEP:

Good shepherds care for their sheep. You must care for the souls of the sheep. You must see that their "souls are restored" to right relationship with God:

> **He restoreth my soul. (Psalms 23:3)**

Caring for sheep includes comforting them in times of sorrow and need. The staff of the shepherd was used to reach out and catch sheep and draw them in close for comfort and examination (Psalms 23:4).

Caring involves directing people to the Good Shepherd who is able to provide all of their needs:

> **The Lord is my shepherd, I shall not want. (Psalms 23:1)**

In speaking of the care of the Lord as his spiritual shepherd, David said:

> **He maketh me to lie down in green pastures: he leadeth me beside the still waters. (Psalm 23:2)**

When sheep are well cared for, they will lie down and be content. Sheep in the natural world, as well as the spiritual world, will lie down only if they are:

Free From Fear: Fear of man or the enemy will scatter the sheep. You must teach the sheep that...

> **God hath not given us the spirit of fear; but of power, and of love, and of a sound mind. (I Timothy 1:7)**

Free From Friction With Other Sheep: Sheep who are fighting each other cannot rest or feed. They also do not reproduce spiritually. When sheep fought in the natural world in Bible times, the shepherd would put oil on their heads. This would make them slick with grease so they could not bump their heads together and fight. Teach the sheep to fight the enemy, not each other. Smear the oil of the Holy Spirit on their heads!

Free Of Pests: In the natural world, there are different types of pests that infest the wool of sheep and cause sickness and discomfort. There are certain flies that attack sheep and leave eggs that hatch, then the baby flies crawl into the head and cause blindness and death.

David said that the shepherd "anointed his head with oil" (Psalm 23:5). In the natural world, shepherds used oil to cleanse the sheep of sickness, disease, and infections. In the spiritual world, pests can be compared to sin. Sin will cause spiritual blindness and death. The oil of the Holy Spirit must be applied to cleanse sheep from the pests of sin.

Free From Hunger And Thirst: If you want sheep to remain in the fold, you must feed them spiritually. The leader must take the sheep to green pastures and feed them with the truth of God's Word:

> **Feed the flock of God which is among you, taking the oversight thereof... (I Peter 5:2)**

It is not enough to just lead people to green pastures. You must make them lie down and abide in them. You must prepare the table with the good things of God and set it before them (Psalms 23:5). You must lead the sheep to the everlasting waters (John 4) that will quench their thirst. Fill their spiritual cups to overflowing with the Word (Psalms 23:5).

In the natural world, if sheep are thirsty they will set out in search of water. If they are not led to good water, they will drink bad water. The shepherd goes before them and checks for poisonous plants growing near streams and for bad water. As a shepherd, you must lead the sheep to good water. Jesus said:

> **If any man thirst, let him come unto me and drink... (John 7:37)**

Jeremiah spoke of "cisterns that hold no water." Emptiness cannot be filled except by the water of life (Jeremiah 2:13).

It is interesting to note in Psalms 23:2 that the shepherd leads to "still waters." Still waters means silent, but running water. Here the water is pure. It is not standing water which is corrupt and filthy. It is fresh. But it is not troubled, nor the rapidly rolling falls which can be dangerous. This speaks of stable doctrine which is not moved by shifting winds of experience or popular theology.

THE SHEPHERD DISCIPLINES THE SHEEP:

Caring for sheep involves discipline. The rod which shepherds carried was used to prod the sheep into the right way. It probably did not feel good to be poked in the side by the rod, but it was necessary.

The rod of the shepherd is a natural example of the rod of the authority of God's Word which is carried by spiritual shepherds. The rod provides discipline. It does not always feel good, but it is necessary.

Leading involves discipline, reproof, and correction to keep sheep on the right path. When a sheep strays, discipline and caring involves going after them and bringing them back to the fold (Luke 15). You must lead sheep from sin into righteousness:

...He leadeth me in the paths of righteousness... (Psalms 23:3)

In the natural world, sheep left to themselves turn to their own ways. They will graze the same area until it is ruined or they will scatter in all directions. The same is true of men and women:

All we like sheep have gone astray; we have turned every one to his own way; and the Lord hath laid on Him the iniquity of us all. (Isaiah 53:6)

By leading men and women in paths of righteousness, you discipline them to the ways of God.

THE SHEPHERD HELPS CAST DOWN SHEEP:

In the natural world, a "cast down" sheep is one that has rolled over on its back and cannot get up by itself. It is an easy prey for animals and it is helpless. The shepherd must come along and prod it with the rod and motivate it to get back up on its feet.

Both sheep and believers become "cast down" when:

They Settle Down In Ease: In the natural world, sheep sometimes become cast down when they get into nice green pasture area and are happy and contented. They roll over on their back, kick their legs in pleasure...and cannot get up again.

In the spiritual world, believers often settle down in material ease. They get involved with pleasures and riches of the world. They are unconcerned about God, His Kingdom, and lost souls. When this happens they become ineffective for God and easy prey for the enemy. To help such sheep, you must focus their attention on eternal values and motivate them for the work of the Kingdom.

They Have Too Much Wool: When the woolly fur of sheep has grown too long, brambles and thorns start clinging to it and the sheep become weighted down with these things, becoming an easy prey for enemies. To help this "cast down" sheep, the shepherd cuts off the trash entangled in the wool. While he is doing it the sheep howls, struggles, and kicks.

In the spiritual world, believers become weighed down with "cares of this world" and the "sins that so easily beset us." These things must be cut off if they are to be effective for God. We may kick, struggle, and howl too, but it is necessary.

They Become Too Fat: Sheep who are too fat cannot right themselves again when they roll over on their backs. Some believers become too fat spiritually. They take in the things of God, but never give out. They do not minister to others, but just continue to grow spiritually fat themselves.

In the natural world, these fat sheep are not always the healthiest or most productive. This is true also in the spiritual world. Spiritual shepherds must get these "fat" sheep up and on the move for God.

THE SHEPHERD LEADS THE SHEEP:

Jesus said:

> **And when he (the shepherd) putteth forth his own sheep, He goeth before them, and the sheep follow him... (John 10:4)**

Leadership is just what the word implies: You must go ahead of the sheep and lead them. You do not just tell sheep where to go, you show them by moving out in front of them. You do this by practicing what you preach and showing them by your lifestyle rather than only telling them. The shepherd sets the example as a leader, not as a "lord" who shows off. Peter said to serve...

> **Neither as being lords over God's heritage, but being ensamples to the flock. (I Peter 5:3)**

THE SHEPHERD SERVES WILLINGLY:

Peter said to...

> **Feed the flock of God which is among you, taking the oversight thereof, not by constraint, but willingly... (I Peter 5:2)**

You should not lead because you are asked, forced, or required to do so. You should lead because you want to lead. Fulfill your calling willingly.

THE SHEPHERD GIVES HIS LIFE FOR THE SHEEP:

Jesus said:

> **I am the good shepherd: the good shepherd giveth His life for the sheep. (John 10:11)**

Jesus was the only sacrifice necessary for the sins of mankind. You cannot die for your sheep in this way. Few of us may ever die in behalf of others or even as martyrs.

But to be a leader, you will have to "give your life" in other ways. You must sacrifice your own desires and selfish ambitions for others. There are many inconveniences in caring for people. It takes time and it may interfere with your own personal plans.

Jesus made this clear in the parable of the lost sheep in Luke 15. All the sheep were obedient and where they were supposed to be, but one was lost. It was not convenient to go out looking for him at night. It was not comfortable or desirable. It was even dangerous. But the shepherd "laid down his life" and went to rescue the lost sheep.

THE SHEPHERD PROTECTS THE SHEEP:

> **The thief cometh not, but for to steal, and to kill, and to destroy... (John 10:10)**
>
> **But he that is an hireling and not the shepherd, whose own the sheep are not, seeth the wolf coming, and leaveth the sheep, and fleeth; and the wolf catcheth them, and scattereth the sheep.**
>
> **The hireling flees, because he is an hireling and careth not for the sheep. (John 10:12-13)**

A good shepherd stays with the sheep and protects them, no matter what the cost.

Hirelings are leaders who use their leadership positions only for money, power, position, or honor. They are serving for "filthy lucre," or their own benefit. Hirelings do not really care for the sheep, so they flee when the enemy attacks (I Peter 5:2).

WARNINGS TO SHEPHERDS

Read Ezekiel 34 in your Bible. This chapter contains warnings to bad shepherds who ruled Israel. But the warnings in this passage concern all leaders who are bad shepherds. God promises "woe" or judgment on shepherds who:

1. Do not feed the flock: Verse 2

2. Rob and take selfishly from the sheep: Verse 3

3. Take care of themselves, but not the sheep: Verses 2-3, 8

4. Do not care for the needs of the flock: Verse 4
   (They do not comfort those who are hurt, strengthen the sheep, care for the spiritually diseased and sick.)

5. Do not seek the lost sheep: Verses 4 and 6

6. Rule with force and cruelty: Verse 4

7. Scatter the sheep: Verses 5-6
8. Let the enemy destroy the sheep: Verse 8
9. Let the diseases of sin and disunity destroy the flock: Verse 21

A PROMISE TO SHEPHERDS

If you are following the Biblical principles of leading like a shepherd, you can claim this promise:

> **...When the chief Shepherd shall appear, ye shall receive a crown of glory that fadeth not away. (I Peter 5:4)**

SELF-TEST

1. Write the Key Verses from memory.

____

____

2. Who is the Good Shepherd?

____

3. What is the one true sheepfold?

____

4. Write a summary of the principles of shepherding which you learned in this lesson. What are the responsibilities of the shepherd?

____

____

____

____

5. Summarize the warnings given to bad shepherds in Ezekiel 34.

____

____

____

____

(Answers to tests are provided at the conclusion of the final chapter in this manual.)

FOR FURTHER STUDY

1. Examine your own life regarding the principles of shepherding which you studied in this lesson. Are you applying these principles in your life and ministry? Where are you failing? How might you improve?

2. Study Psalm 23 using this outline. As a shepherd, the Lord is your:

-Provider:	Psalm 23:1
-Peace:	Psalm 23:2
-Path-maker:	Psalm 23:3
-Protection:	Psalm 23:4
-Preparation:	Psalm 23:5
-Plenty (cup runs over):	Psalm 23:5
-Promise:	Psalm 23:6

Additional notes on Psalm 23: In speaking of goodness and mercy in verse 6, note the...

-Closeness of it:	"It shall follow me."
-Continuance of it:	It will continue throughout life.
-Constancy of it:	"All the days" means constantly.
-Certainty of it:	"Surely."

Consider this question: Do goodness and mercy follow you? As you pass through life do you leave behind you encouragement, inspiration, mercy, and goodness?

In speaking of the valley, which illustrates hard times in our Christian experience, note that...

-It is in reality nothing but a shadow. When you see a shadow in the natural world, there is something else that causes it. The shadow is not the reality. In the spiritual world, it is the warfare of the enemy that is behind every shadow in our valleys.

-It is a walk "through." You will not be in the valley forever. It does not say "I died there" or "I stayed there."

-It is a "walk," not a fearful run.

-It is valleys in the natural world that are the most fruitful areas. The question is not whether or not you will go through a valley. You will go through many. The question is, how will you react to them? Will you feed on the good things of God that grow only in valleys?

-Both the shepherd's rod (for discipline) and staff (for caring) are at work in our valley experiences.

3. Learn more about what the Bible teaches regarding shepherding by studying the following references:

-Numbers 27:17
-Psalms 23; 80:1
-Isaiah 40:11
-Ezekiel 34; 37:24
-Zechariah 10:2; 11:15-17
-Matthew 9:36; 25:32; 26:31
-Mark 6:34; 14:27
-John 10
-Hebrews 13:20
-I Peter 2:25; 5:4

CHAPTER SEVEN

TASKS OF LEADERS

OBJECTIVES:

Upon completion of this chapter you will be able to:

- Write the Key Verses from memory.
- Identify the priority task of leaders.
- Define "perfecting."
- Summarize the results of "perfecting" people for the work of the ministry.
- Identify specific tasks of leaders.

KEY VERSES:

> **And He (God) gave some apostles; and some, prophets; and some, evangelists; and some, pastors and teachers; For the perfecting of the saints for the work of the ministry, for the edifying of the body of Christ. (Ephesians 4:11-12)**

INTRODUCTION

In previous lessons you learned HOW you should lead as a good steward, servant, and shepherd. This and following lessons focus on WHAT a leader actually does.

Leadership involves many tasks. A task is a responsibility, duty, or job. There is no way we can discuss every task a leader may be called upon to do, so we will consider only the major tasks of leaders.

THE FIRST PRIORITY

The first priority of a Christian leader is defined in the following passage:

> **And He (God) gave some apostles; and some, prophets; and some, evangelists; and some, pastors and teachers;**
>
> **For the perfecting of the saints for the work of the ministry, for the edifying of the body of Christ. (Ephesians 4:11-12)**

God sets leaders in the Church to "perfect" believers for the work of the ministry. This word "perfect" means to prepare or equip. The "work of the ministry" includes every position, duty, and responsibility of ministry.

The main task of Christian leaders is to perfect believers for the work of the ministry. Because every believer is given at least one spiritual gift, leaders have a great resource from which to draw. Each believer must be equipped spiritually to do the work for which God has called him.

Perfecting involves teaching, preaching, demonstrating, and training. Perfecting also involves mobilizing people for the work of the ministry. To "mobilize" is to activate or put into action. Believers must not only be trained, but they must be mobilized to use what they have learned.

Perfecting involves training some people as leaders and others as followers. All are important to the work of the ministry. Chapter Ten of this course is devoted to training leaders and followers.

If you are a leader called and chosen by God you should be involved in equipping others to do God's work. This is your first priority and your main task. These are the positive results when believers are properly "perfected" for the work of the ministry:

-The work of the ministry is done: Ephesians 4:12
-The Body of Christ (the Church) is edified (built up): Ephesians 4:12
-People reach spiritual maturity: Ephesians 4:13-15
-Unity results: Ephesians 4:13
-People are conformed into the image of Christ: Ephesians 4:13
-People become stable doctrinally, grounded in the truth: Ephesians 4:15-16
-The Body of Christ functions effectively: Ephesians 4:16

RESPONSIBILITIES OF THE PERFECTING PROCESS

This "perfecting" of believers involves many responsibilities. Here are some of them:

SETTING THE EXAMPLE:

We have already discussed in detail the responsibility of leaders to set a proper example to followers. As an example, the leader must be called, anointed, a good steward and shepherd, and a servant of all. His life must evidence the qualifications for leaders discussed in Chapter Four. He must be a man of prayer and a student of God's Word. Your example must be godly, because...

> **A disciple is not above his teacher, but everyone who is perfectly trained will be like his teacher. (Luke 6:40)**

The ability to manage and lead others begins with proper management of self. You must set an example in personal conduct and discipline, in relationship with God, and in evangelism and every "work of the ministry."

CARING:

Another major responsibility of leaders is to care for followers. This was already stressed in the lessons on leading like a shepherd and a servant. People, not plans or projects, are most important.

As a leader, you are called of God to care for the followers with whom God entrusts you. You must love them, be concerned about their problems, and minister to their spiritual, physical, and material needs as God enables. An important part of caring is for a leader to pray for his followers. Do not sin against God by failing to pray for those entrusted to your care.

LEADING:

A leader must lead and guide. He provides direction to people to enable them to accomplish the ministry to which they are called. You must guide people where God wants them to go, not where they selfishly desire to wander. Leading involves counseling people to walk in God's ways by guiding them with Scriptural principles.

DECISION MAKING:

To lead others, you are required to make many decisions. There are some basic principles of decision making that can assist you in this task. You will study these in Chapter Eight.

HANDLING CONFLICTS AND DISCIPLINES:

Whenever you work with a group of people, conflicts always arise. A leader must be able to solve such conflicts with guidance of the Lord. There will also be people who need spiritual discipline because they fall into doctrinal error or sin and need correction. Chapter Nine of this course provides guidelines for handling tasks of conflict and discipline.

ANALYZING THE ENVIRONMENT:

To be effective, you must understand the people to whom you are ministering. You must understand their problems, needs, and concerns. To gain such understanding, you analyze their "environment" which includes their spiritual, physical, material, and cultural situations. The Harvestime International Institute course, *"Environmental Analysis,"* details principles of analyzing the environment for ministry purposes.

IDENTIFYING PURPOSE:

Purpose is basically spiritual vision. The Bible says:

> **Where there is no vision, the people perish... (Proverbs 29:18)**

Purpose, or spiritual vision, involves understanding two things:

1. The purposes of God.
2. Your part in fulfilling His purpose and plans.

When you identify your purpose in ministry, you discover your personal part in God's plan. Purpose establishes a vision or goal for ministry. It provides direction and understanding of exactly what your ministry is called of God to accomplish. It permits you to plan and implement plans to accomplish your purpose. When you clearly understand God's purpose and your part in it, you can effectively lead others.

The Harvestime International Institute course, *"Management By Objectives,"* will help you identify your purpose in God's plan.

PLANNING:

Knowing your purpose of ministry is not the same as accomplishing your purpose. You must make and implement plans to accomplish it. You must add action to knowledge and works to faith in order to accomplish the work of the ministry. Planning under the direction of the Holy Spirit permits you to work in harmony with God to accomplish His plans and purposes.

You must make specific plans to accomplish your own purpose of ministry. If you are a leader, you help followers make plans to accomplish the work of the corporate or group ministry. Planning involves deciding...

-What you are going to do.
-How you are going to do it (the methods or action steps).
-When you are going to do it.
-Who is going to do it.
-The cost of doing it.
-A method to evaluate and see if it has been done as you planned.

Planning is a major task of leaders. It is a Biblical principle and is discussed in detail in the Harvestime International Institute course entitled *"Management By Objectives."*

IMPLEMENTING PLANS:

After a leader has made plans, these plans must be implemented or put into action. To implement a plan, the leader must perform the following tasks. Each of these is discussed in detail in the course entitled *"Management By Objectives"*:

-Selecting people to fulfill the plan.

-Communicating to them the plan, the work of the ministry to be done.

-Delegating the authority and responsibility to accomplish the plan.

-Training those selected in the skills necessary to accomplish the work.

-Organizing the people involved and details of the plan.

-Scheduling starting and completion dates and periodic checks on the progress of the plan.

-Budgeting the funds necessary to accomplish the plan.

-Making decisions.

-Reviewing progress.

-Evaluating the work of the ministry. Evaluation determines if you fulfilled the plan and if it really contributed to accomplishing God's purposes for your ministry.

STRENGTHENED FOR THE TASK

As previously stated, there is no way to discuss every task which a leader may have to perform, but the ones mentioned are the major responsibilities of every leader. Here is a promise to claim for these tasks and every other responsibility you may be called upon to fulfill in leadership:

> **I can do all things through Christ which strengtheneth me. (Philippians 4:13)**

Whenever you get under pressure and begin to think, "There is no way I can do all that needs to be done," you need to spend more time alone with God. You will not become tired and frustrated if you take time to wait on God:

> **Thou wilt keep him in perfect peace, whose mind is stayed on thee; because he trusteth in thee. (Isaiah 26:3)**

Pray this "leader's prayer" prayed by King Solomon:

And thy servant is in the midst of thy people which thou hast chosen, a great people, that cannot be numbered nor counted for multitude.

Give therefore thy servant an understanding heart to judge thy people, that I may discern between good and bad: for who is able to judge this thy so great a people? (I Kings 3:8-9)

SELF-TEST

1. Write the Key Verses from memory.

____

____

2. What is the priority task of leaders?

____

3. Define "perfecting."

____

4. What are the positive results of "perfecting" people for the work of the ministry?

____

____

____

5. Summarize major responsibilities of leaders who perfect believers for the work of the ministry.

____

____

____

____

____

(Answers to tests are provided at the conclusion of the final chapter in this manual.)

FOR FURTHER STUDY

1. Several references were made in this chapter to the Harvestime International Institute courses, *"Environmental Analysis"* and *"Management By Objectives."* As mentioned in the beginning of this course, we suggest you obtain these two courses to continue your study of Biblical management.

2. Here are some Biblical examples which illustrate some of the tasks of leaders:

REBUILDING THE WALLS OF JERUSALEM

THE PROBLEM:

Nehemiah received a report that the remnant in Judah who had returned were in great distress and reproached because the walls of Jerusalem were broken down and burned with fire: Nehemiah 1:2-3

THE SOLUTION:

Nehemiah fasted and prayed: Nehemiah 1:4-11

He revealed his sadness to the king: Nehemiah 2:1-2

He told the king why he was depressed: Nehemiah 2:3

The king asked, "What is your request?": Nehemiah 2:4

Nehemiah asked God for guidance in answering this question: Nehemiah 2:4

He asked the king to send him to Judah to rebuild the walls: Nehemiah 2:5

The king responded positively: Nehemiah 2:6

Nehemiah asked the king for official letters so he could travel freely and obtain timber from the forests: Nehemiah 2:7-8

When Nehemiah arrived he spent three nights secretly surveying the problem and developed a strategy for rebuilding: Nehemiah 2:12-16
Nehemiah then revealed his plan and asked the people to help him rebuild the walls: Nehemiah 2:17-3:32

When the enemies of Israel tried to stop the work, the people prayed and set a guard: Nehemiah 4:1-13

When the people grew fearful, Nehemiah encouraged them: Nehemiah 4:14

As a soon as the word got out to the enemy that they were ready to defend themselves, they returned to building: Nehemiah 4:15

Nehemiah devised a new plan for working and guarding so they could continue building: 4:16-23

THE RESULTS:

They completed the walls in 52 days: Nehemiah 6:15

The people praised God: Nehemiah 12:27-29, 31-42

The people purified themselves and the city: Nehemiah 12:30

They offered sacrifices to God: Nehemiah 12:43

When the enemies of Israel witnessed this victory and heard the rejoicing, they lost their confidence: Nehemiah 6:16

DOCTRINAL ERRORS

THE PROBLEM:

Certain men were teaching false doctrines in Antioch: Acts 15:1

Paul and Barnabas could not solve the problem: Acts 15:2

THE SOLUTION:

The church at Antioch decided to seek guidance from the apostles and elders at Jerusalem: Acts 15:2-3

The Antioch delegation reported how Gentiles were being converted through faith alone: Acts 15:4

The apostles and elders met in a closed session to discuss the matter: Acts 15:6

Peter reminded the people of what God did for Cornelius and his household: Acts 15:7-11

Paul and Barnabas gave specific testimony regarding the things God had done through them among the Gentiles: Acts 15:12

James recalled how the Old Testament prophets had predicted Gentile conversion: Acts 15:13-18

James proposed a solution to the problem: Acts 15:19-21

The apostles, elders, and the whole church agreed to the proposal: Acts 15:22

A letter was written: Acts 15:22-30

Judas and Silas were chosen to deliver the letter: Acts 15:22

Judas and Silas delivered the letter and also a message: Acts 15:30,32

THE RESULTS:

The congregation rejoiced: Acts 15:31

Judas and Silas were sent back to Jerusalem in peace: Acts 15:33

The work of God continued unhindered: Acts 15:35

Instructions in the letters were delivered by Paul, Silas, and Timothy to other new churches: Acts 16:4-5

JUDGING THE PEOPLE

THE PROBLEM:

The people stood about Moses from morning until evening for him to solve their problems: Exodus 18:13

Moses tried to do the job all by himself: Exodus 18:14-16

This process caused problems for both Moses and the people: Exodus 18:18

THE SOLUTION:

Jethro advised Moses to establish priorities: Exodus 18:19

He formulated a plan for delegation: Exodus 18:19-22

Moses communicated the problem to the people: Deuteronomy 1:9-12

Moses instructed each tribe to choose wise men and he appointed them as leaders: Deuteronomy 1:13

Moses carefully instructed the leaders in their responsibilities: Deuteronomy 1:16-18

THE RESULTS:

Moses was assisted in leadership responsibilities: Exodus 18:22

Moses was able to endure the demands of his leadership role: Exodus 18:23

NEGLECTED WIDOWS

THE PROBLEM:

The disciples were increasing rapidly and with such growth, the communal system was put under stress. Certain widows were being overlooked and began to complain: Acts 6:1

The apostles got involved in the details of this problem and it caused them to neglect their primary responsibility of teaching God's Word: Acts 6:2

THE SOLUTION:

A meeting of all the believers was called: Acts 6:2

The people were informed regarding the major tasks of the 12 apostles, which was prayer and ministry of the Word: Acts 6:3-4

The people were told to select seven qualified men to care for the needs that existed: Acts 6:3

The people chose seven men: Acts 6:5

The apostles confirmed their choice through prayer and the laying on of hands: Acts 6:6

THE RESULTS:

The needs of the people were met and unity was restored. The apostles were able to fulfill their primary work: Acts 6:7

CHAPTER EIGHT

DECISION-MAKING

OBJECTIVES:

Upon completion of this chapter you will be able to:

- Write the Key Verse from memory.
- Explain the Biblical approach to decision-making.
- Summarize guidelines for decision-making.
- Explain the purpose of a model.
- Explain the value of a model in decision-making.
- Use a Biblical model for decision making

KEY VERSE:

> **A man's heart deviseth his way; but the Lord directeth his steps. (Proverbs 16:9)**

INTRODUCTION

Making decisions is a difficult task facing leaders each day. Each decision is important, because decisions on small matters over a period of time affect your entire life and ministry.

A decision is a choice. You must find an answer for a real life situation and decide what action you will take. Decisions determine destiny. Decisions made by a leader affect not only his destiny, but the destiny of his followers.

Life is an endless succession of choices and decisions. Making choices is a responsibility. Refusing to make a decision is in itself a decision. This lesson presents guidelines for making good decisions and a Biblical model for decision-making.

THE BIBLICAL APPROACH

The Biblical approach to decision making is not voting by the people. It is not the democratic approach or "majority rule." The problems of this approach are illustrated by the story of Israel at the border of Canaan (see Numbers 13).

Democratic process in the Church produces compromise, legalism, and competition. Rules of order, motions, and votes limit revelation by the Holy Spirit. Voting often results in hurt feelings, anger, and church splits. These are not Biblical ways of decision-making for the Church. They are methods the Church has adopted from democratic government styles of the world.

Acts chapter 15 is an excellent example of a Biblical approach to decision-making. This example concerned a problem of Jewish customs. To solve it, the leaders met, prayed, examined the facts, and arrived at an agreement under the direction of the Holy Spirit.

God sets leaders in the Church to make decisions. He gives them wisdom to fulfill this responsibility. When there is a decision to be made, leaders should meet together, pray, examine the facts, and arrive at an agreement under the direction of the Holy Spirit.

GUIDELINES FOR MAKING DECISIONS

Here are some guidelines to help leaders make good decisions:

1. IDENTIFY THE PROBLEM:

What is the issue, problem or question that requires a decision? Gather all the available information concerning the matter. State the problem in a brief written statement. You cannot make the right decision if you have not identified the right problem.

2. FOLLOW THE MODEL FOR DECISION MAKING:

A model is an example of something. It provides an example for you to follow. A model for decision making provides an example to follow when making decisions. On the next page is a Biblical model that will help you make wise choices within the will of God. Look at the model, then read the explanation which follows:

A BIBLICAL MODEL FOR DECISION MAKING

Identify the problem, question, or life situation for which guidance is sought.

Is it dealt with in Scripture by specific command, general principle or example?

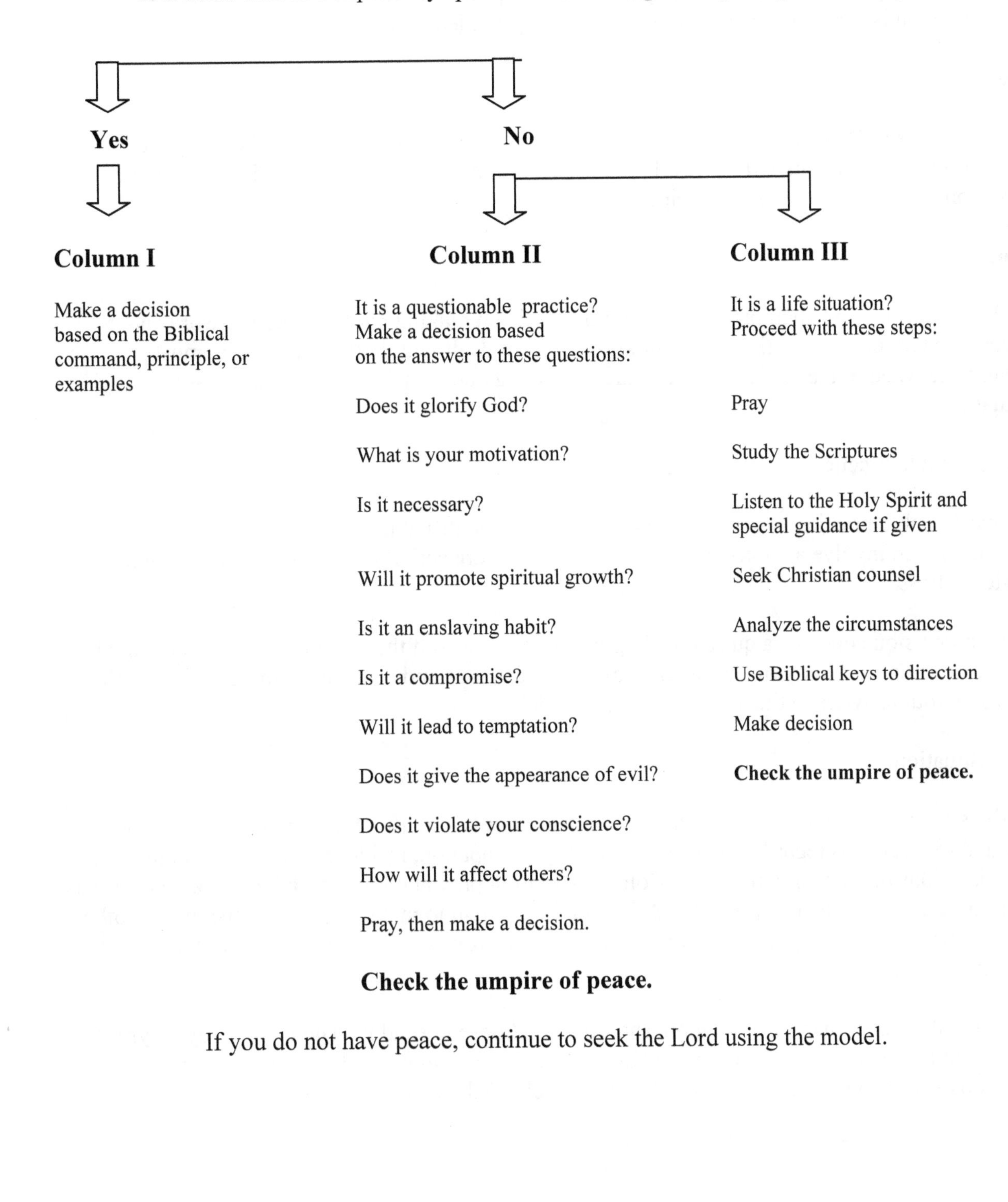

USING THE MODEL:

The first step in the decision-making model is to identify the problem, question, or life situation for which guidance is sought. Next, search the written Word of God to determine if the problem is dealt with by commandment, example, or general principle. Guidance for many decisions, especially on issues of right and wrong, is already provided in the Bible.

Yes:

If the answer is "Yes, the problem is dealt with in the written Word of God" then make the decision based upon this written revelation. (See Column I on the model.) Make sure your decision is in harmony with the Scriptures.

No:

If the answer is "no," then proceed on with the decision making model under the word "no." There are two choices on the model for situations not dealt with in the Bible. You must determine whether the decision to be made involves a questionable practice or a real life situation.

Questionable Practice:

A questionable practice is something not specifically identified in Scripture as either right or wrong. It can involve a choice of entertainment or leisure activities, a habit, food and drinks, or style of dress.

If your decision concerns a questionable practice, ask yourself the questions listed on the model under Column II. After you answer each of these questions and pray, make the decision on the basis of your answers to the questions on the model.

Life Situation:

A life situation is a major choice which can affect your future life. It can include, but is not limited to, decisions regarding marriage, ministry, occupation, residence, choice of churches, etc. For decisions on life situations, use Column III. First pray about the decision. Ask God for His will to be accomplished in your life. Ask Him for wisdom to make the right decision. Ask others to pray with you. Study the Scriptures and claim the promises for direction given in the written Word of God.

Acknowledge supernatural revelation, should God choose to send it. There are many ways God speaks to men supernaturally to reveal His will and help them make decisions. These include methods such as visions, prophecies, dreams, angels, and an audible voice.

But such supernatural revelation is the exception rather than the rule. One of the purposes of the Holy Spirit in the life of the believer is to provide guidance:

> **Howbeit when He, the Spirit of truth, is come, He will guide you into all truth: for He shall not speak of Himself, but whatsoever He shall hear, that shall He speak; and He will shew you things to come. (John 16:13)**

The Lord most often guides in this way. If supernatural revelation is given, praise God! But always remember...No dream, vision, prophecy, or other revelation is of God if it conflicts with His written Word.

Another Biblical method which aids decision-making is Christian counsel. Wise counsel from spiritual leaders is important:

> **Where no counsel is, the people fall; but in the multitude of counselors there is safety. (Proverbs 11:14)**

> **The way of a fool is right in his own eyes; but he that hearkeneth unto counsel is wise. (Proverbs 12:15)**

You should also analyze the circumstances affecting the decision and use the Biblical keys for direction given in Proverbs 3:5-6.

3. IDENTIFY VARIOUS OPTIONS:

When you follow the model for decision making, you may discover several different solutions to the problem you face. Identify various options and evaluate each possible solution on the basis of:

The Risks: Balance faith with common sense and reality. Evaluate the advantages and disadvantages of each possible solution. Open and closed doors of circumstances may affect your decision.

The Resources: Do you have the needed resources to implement a certain solution? No decision will be better than the people who must carry it out. No decision will be implemented if you do not have or cannot trust God to provide the necessary financial resources.

The Results: Which solution will give the greatest results with the least effort? There is no reason to do things the hard way. If there is an easier way to achieve the same results, choose it (unless God should reveal otherwise).

4. SELECT THE BEST SOLUTION:

After you have examined all possible solutions, select the best one. You have asked God to guide you, so believe that He will. You normally should select the solution that is best in terms of risks, resources, and results.

We say "normally," because sometimes God leads in a way that does not appear best to natural thinking. Remember that God's ways are not your ways. Sometimes His plan may not seem best to natural reasoning, so be open to this.

There is a certain amount of risk in every decision unless God speaks directly to you through His Word or divine revelation. Do not be afraid of making the wrong decision. Most wrong decisions can be corrected.

Remember that the Holy Spirit guides your decisions:

> **A man's heart deviseth his way; but the Lord directeth his steps. (Proverbs 16:9)**

When you make a decision and you do not have peace in your spirit, continue to seek the Lord using the steps on the model. Inner peace is one of the ways the Holy Spirit confirms right decisions. Do not make a final decision until you have the peace of God confirming your choice.

5. COMMUNICATE THE DECISION:

Let people know the decision you have made. Communicate it clearly before you act upon it.

6. IMPLEMENT THE DECISION:

Once the decision is made, implement it (put it into action) and then go on to something else. You gain nothing by worrying about past decisions. Instead, after a period of time evaluate the decision.

7. EVALUATE THE DECISION:

Evaluate the decision you made. Did it solve the problem? Is it a good decision? Is God blessing it? Do you need to make a change? Most decisions can be changed if necessary. Many decisions can be improved. Be flexible and open to change as directed by the Holy Spirit.

A FINAL WORD OF CAUTION

Never make a decision when you are angry, upset, or under pressure. Do not make decisions too quickly. Take time to hear the facts. Most decisions do not have to be made immediately. It is Satan who pushes and causes panic and hurry. The Holy Spirit leads gently. Never be in a hurry in the decision-making process:

> **Wait on the Lord; be of good courage, and He shall strengthen thine heart: wait, I say, on the Lord. (Psalms 27:14)**
>
> **My soul, wait thou only upon God; for my expectation is from him. (Psalms 62:5)**
>
> **Rest in the Lord, and wait patiently for Him... (Psalms 37:7)**
>
> **But they that wait upon the Lord shall renew their strength; they shall mount up with wings as eagles; they shall run, and not be weary; and they shall walk, and not faint. (Isaiah 40:31)**

SELF-TEST

1. Write the Key Verse from memory.

____

____

2. What is the Biblical approach to decision-making? Is it voting and majority rule?

____

3. Summarize the seven guidelines for decision-making given in this lesson.

____

____

____

____

____

____

____

4. What is a model for decision-making?

____

5. What is the purpose of a model?

____

(Answers to tests are provided at the conclusion of the final chapter in this manual.)

FOR FURTHER STUDY

1. Here is a sample problem and decision:

The Problem:

There are not enough Sunday school teachers. Few people are willing to serve as substitutes. In several cases, classes have been combined. Attendance is decreasing.

Possible Solutions:

1. Appeal for volunteers.
2. Combine more classes.
3. Start a training program to train new teachers.

Analyzing Solutions:

1. Appealing for volunteers will make more people available to teach, but will these people be properly trained?

2. Combining more classes may solve the problem of lack of teachers. But will the students get personal attention in such large classes? Will the quality of small group relationships be lost?

3. A training program will provide new teachers who are prepared to substitute or take classes.

Selecting The Best Solution:

Option 3 is best. The training program will provide a continued source of new teachers who are properly prepared to teach. You might use options 1 (volunteers) and 2 (combining classes) until the first group of teachers is trained.

Evaluation:

After three months, evaluate the decision. Is the training program solving the problem of lack of teachers?

2. Think of a decision with which you are faced. Use the principles you learned in this lesson to help you make a choice.

3. The Bible is a history of decisions made by individuals and nations in relation to God's will. For further study of making decisions and the will of God obtain the Harvestime International Institute course, *"Knowing God's Voice."*

4. Read about King Rehoboam who took bad advice when faced with a decision: I Kings 12:1-19

CHAPTER NINE

CONFLICTS AND DISCIPLINE

OBJECTIVES:

Upon completion of this chapter you will be able to:

- Write the Key Verses from memory.
- Identify the true reason for all conflicts.
- Summarize ways to prevent conflict.
- Summarize guidelines for dealing with conflict.
- Identify reasons why discipline is necessary.
- Summarize Scriptural principles of discipline.

KEY VERSES:

> **All Scripture is given by inspiration of God, and is profitable for doctrine, for reproof, for correction, for instruction in righteousness:**
>
> **That the man of God may be perfect, thoroughly furnished unto all good works. (II Timothy 3:16-17)**

INTRODUCTION

In Chapter Seven you studied about tasks of leaders. Two important tasks of every leader are providing discipline and solving conflicts. Whenever you work with and minister to people these tasks are necessary. Discipline is correction of those who are wrong. A conflict is a fight or quarrel. A good leader must provide correction and be able to solve problems between his followers.

DISAGREEING WITHOUT CONFLICT

People can disagree without having conflict, but conflict often results from disagreements. It is not differences of opinion that hurt and destroy, but the failure to love when we have them.

Paul and Barnabas had a disagreement over Mark in Acts 15:36-41. This disagreement did not lead to hostility and hatred. The problem was solved by forming a second evangelistic team. This solution actually advanced the spread of the Gospel. Paul and Barnabas did not get angry, stop speaking, and have nothing more to do with one another. Neither one dropped out of Christian service because "someone had hurt them." They both continued on to serve the Lord.

When people are fighting each other, they are not fighting Satan. God wants leaders to deal with conflict and discipline effectively so the work of His Kingdom can proceed.

THE ROLE OF GOD'S WORD

God's Word has an important role in solving discipline problems and conflicts:

> **All Scripture is given by inspiration of God, and is profitable for doctrine, for reproof, for correction, for instruction in righteousness:**
>
> **That the man of God may be perfect, thoroughly furnished unto all good works. (II Timothy 3:16-17)**

When we discipline and solve conflicts on the basis of God's Word, people are perfected and equipped for the work of the ministry. God's Word is effective for discipline, reproof, and correction.

A BIBLICAL PATTERN

Any time a church, organization, or work of God is launched, it goes through certain stages of development. Here is an example of these stages. Read the following chapters in your Bible:

Acts 1	God chose certain men.
Acts 2	He gave these men a ministry.
Acts 3	There was great multiplication.
Acts 4	A great movement was born (the Church).
Acts 5-6	Discipline and conflict arose.

In Acts 1-4 a great work of God is birthed, then in Acts 5:1-11, a discipline problem arises. Peter does not ignore it, but confronts and deals with it. In Acts 5:12-42, conflict from without the Church arises. The disciples stand in the face of opposition and boldly declare:

> **We ought to obey God rather than men...And daily, in the temple and in every house, they ceased not to teach and preach Jesus Christ. (Acts 5:29 and 42)**

In Acts 6:1, conflict from within the church arises. There is a dispute over the distribution of supplies to widows. Again, the disciples immediately solve the conflict. They could have just silenced the complaints by saying, "If you were spiritual you would not be complaining."

They also could have said, "Do not challenge the leadership God has appointed. Submit or split!" Instead, they had the attitude of a good leader. They said, "We hear you have a problem. Let us see if together, with God's help, we can solve it." (See Acts 6:2-7.)

Anytime a ministry or work of God is launched, it will experience this same pattern. There will be discipline problems and conflicts from without and within. Satan wants to destroy the work of the ministry.

You must also remember that one who is being led by the Spirit will usually come into conflict with others who are being led (at least for a time) by the flesh. (See the conflicts of Jesus in the "For Further Study" section of this lesson.)

A good leader does not ignore such difficult situations. He does not call people "unspiritual" for bringing problems to his attention. He immediately deals with issues of discipline and conflict.

THE TRUE REASON FOR CONFLICTS

The Bible reveals the true reason behind conflicts between believers and in the Church and Christian ministries:

> **But if ye have bitter envying and strife in your hearts, glory not, and lie not against the truth.**
>
> **This wisdom descendeth not from above, but is earthly, sensual, devilish.**
>
> **For where envying and strife is there is confusion and every evil work. (James 3:14-16)**
>
> **From whence come wars and fightings among you? Come they not hence, even of your lusts that war in your members? (James 4:1.)**
>
> **For ye are yet carnal: for whereas there is among you envying, and strife, and division, are ye not carnal, and walk as men? (I Corinthians 3:3)**

Conflicts arise because of spiritually immature and carnal Christians motivated by Satan, the flesh, and pride.

PREVENTING CONFLICT

The best way to handle conflict is to prevent it before it occurs. Here are some ways to prevent conflict:

1. Raise up spiritually mature believers (James 3:14-16; 4:1; I Corinthians 3:3).

2. Keep people well informed. Confusion and lack of information create problems. Build strong bridges of communication between those involved with you in the work of the ministry. Good leaders in the Bible (like Moses, Nehemiah, Ezra, etc.) were good communicators.

3. Whenever you are doing a work for God, there will always be problems. Let people know you expect problems, that you are not surprised when they arise, and that you know you will be able to solve them through the power of the Holy Spirit.

4. Think ahead. By careful planning you can deal with many problems before they become conflicts.

5. Build strong relationships. Say only good about others, and train those who work with you in ministry to speak well of others.

6. Give sincere appreciation and credit to those who work with you in ministry.

7. If you make a mistake, be big enough to admit and correct it.

8. Be clear in your purpose and plans of ministry. If everyone knows what you are doing and why, there is less opportunity for misunderstanding and conflict.

9. When it is necessary to set rules, establish clear rules and communicate them immediately to others.

10. Be available to your co-workers so you will be aware of problems when they arise. Without your attention, simple problems can turn into big conflicts.

11. Operate the ministry on Biblical principles, the greatest of which is love.

DEALING WITH CONFLICT

When a problem or conflict does arise, follow these guidelines:

1. Make yourself available to deal with it. You cannot handle problems if you are never around.

2. Pray for wisdom to deal with the problem.

3. Determine the real problem. The conflict is not the real problem. What caused the conflict is the problem. To determine the problem you must ask questions, observe, and continue to pray for revelation. Listen to all sides of the problem and to all people involved. Do not act without a clear understanding of all the facts. Always keep in mind the real source of problems (James 3:14-16; 4:1; I Corinthians 3:3).

4. Let people who are directly affected by the problem suggest solutions. Be willing to listen to all suggestions. Pray together about a solution. In serious conflicts, fasting is also recommended.

5. If the conflict is a personal problem between two people, bring them together following the principles of Matthew 18:15-17.

6. Deal with conflicts with a proper attitude. Be forgiving, seeking to restore rather than sever relationships. Be loving. Do not threaten or become angry. Do not allow people to yell or say bad things about each other.

   Use tact. Tact is the ability to deal with difficult situations with wisdom and love without offending people. It involves being sensitive to others, being understanding, and using words that restore and heal rather than divide and wound. Be flexible. Do not be selfishly set on having your own way. Be open to different ideas and ways of solving problems.

7. Deal with one conflict or problem at a time. Do not confuse the issue by discussing other related problems.

8. When you have a clear understanding of the problem causing the conflict, act immediately to correct it. Remember that a solution should always advance the Kingdom of God. Turn conflicts into cooperation, as in the example of Paul and Barnabas.

9. Explain why you are handling the conflict the way you are. For example, in the church conflict described in Acts 15, the leaders explained their decision in detail in writing to those involved.

10. Thank God for the problem and what you learned from the experience. When you give thanks in "everything," it releases the divine energy and power of God to work on your behalf.

REASONS FOR DISCIPLINE

It is the nature of sin to rebel against authority. This is what caused the original sin of Lucifer (the Devil) and of man (Adam and Eve). Because of this basic sin nature, you will sometimes have to lead those who may not want to be led. You will have followers who fall into rebellion, sin, and evidence spiritual carnality and immaturity.

The pastor or spiritual leader has the authority for discipline within a Church or ministry because he has the responsibility for the spiritual welfare of followers:

> **Obey them that have the rule over you, and submit yourselves; for they watch for your souls, as they that must give account, that they may do it with joy, and not with grief; for that is unprofitable for you. (Hebrews 13:17)**

The leader must be willing to handle discipline problems immediately when they occur. To allow spiritual failure or sin to go unchallenged can be fatal to any ministry. Here are some Scriptural reasons for discipline:

1. To restore a person who is denying the Word of God or who has given reason for offense: Galatians 6:1; Matthew 6:14-15

2. To correct sin: I Corinthians 8:9

3. To protect the Christian testimony of the Church: I Timothy 3:7

4. To encourage members to remain faithful in their witness and not to become careless: I Corinthians 5:6-7

PRINCIPLES OF DISCIPLINE

Here are some guidelines for discipline:

1. Go first to the erring brother and solve the matter individually and personally if possible: Luke 17:3; Matthew 18:15-17.

2. If the erring believer will not listen to you and repent, go again with witnesses: Matthew 18:15-17.

3. If he still refuses to hear you, take the matter before the entire Church: Matthew 18:15-17

4. Discipline should be done by leaders with a proper spirit. See Matthew 7:1-5; Romans 15:1-2; II Corinthians 2:6-8, and Galatians 6:1-4. Spiritually mature believers are to first judge themselves and then deal with offenders with a spirit of meekness, love, and helpfulness.

5. Correction should be done with the purpose of restoring the offender who has been taken captive by Satan: II Timothy 2:24-26.

6. If correction is refused, discipline may include exclusion from the fellowship. One of the greatest gifts God has given believers is fellowship with others believers. One of the most severe punishments is withholding such fellowship. See Matthew 18:15-17; I Corinthians 5; II Thessalonians 3:14; II John 7-11; and III John 9-11.

7. Opportunity should be given for the erring brother to respond. His attitude should affect the discipline and his future in ministry. If his attitude is good and he repents, the leader can restore him to fellowship and ministry. If the offense is serious, the offender may need to be removed from active ministry until he sets his own life and home in order. If

he is rebellious and does not repent, he must be removed from leadership positions, and possibly, the church fellowship.

8. Private problems and public sins should be handled differently. See Matthew 18:15-17; I Corinthians 5; Galatians 2:1-14; I Timothy 5:20. In the passage from Matthew it seems the problem was between private individuals. It was to be dealt with by enlisting the aid of other believers and, if the offender would not listen, by excluding him from fellowship. In the other passages, the problems were matters of public record so they had to be dealt with publicly.

9. Exercise discipline only on the basis of factual knowledge. "Hearsay" evidence is not sufficient. There must also be two or three witnesses. See Matthew 18:15-18; I Corinthians 5:1 and I Timothy 5:1,9.

A RULE TO REMEMBER

A good rule to remember when you must discipline others is...

Whatever you wish that men would do to you, do so to them.
(Matthew 7:12) Revised Standard Version

Always ask yourself:

1. "What does God's Word say about this?"
2. "How would Jesus handle this?"
3. "How would I want to be treated in this situation if our positions were reversed and I was him and he was me?"

SELF-TEST

1. Write the Key Verses from memory.

2. List some ways to prevent conflict.

3. Summarize guidelines for dealing with conflict.

4. List some Biblical reasons for exercising discipline.

5. Summarize Scriptural principles of discipline which you learned in this lesson.

6. What is the true reason for conflict?

7. Why is God's Word important in discipline?

(Answers to tests are provided at the conclusion of the final chapter in this manual.)

FOR FURTHER STUDY

1. Here are some common reasons for discipline within a Church or Christian organization. A brother or sister....

   -Is immoral (sexual sins, adultery, pornography, fornication).
   -Is dishonest with ministry funds, personal finances or business.
   -Is untruthful.
   -Cannot work with other people.
   -Has wrong attitudes of rebellion, criticism, and hatred.
   -Is worldly, carnal, and spiritually immature.
   -Sets a bad example in his conduct and lifestyle.
   -Is not fulfilling the responsibilities of his leadership position.
   -Does not believe God's Word.
   -Talks about others and stirs up trouble.

   Can you think of other reasons?

2. Sometimes leaders experience conflicts with their followers because they cannot handle criticism. A critic is one who does not agree with the way you are doing things and tells you so. Honest criticism given in love can be helpful. It can help you improve. But you will also experience unjust criticism.

   Here are some suggestions for handling criticism:

   -Be a good listener. Listen to what the critic has to say.

   -Thank him for bringing a matter to your attention and say, "I will investigate and pray about this matter."

   -Pray about the criticism. Ask God to show you if it is a matter of real concern that should be corrected.

   -Investigate: Did you make a wrong decision? Are you doing wrong? Accumulate facts on which to base your decision.

   -If you find the criticism is unjust, ignore it. If it is a just criticism of a problem or failure, correct the situation.

3. Jesus faced much conflict during His earthly ministry. Study how He dealt with conflicts...

-Between His followers over position: Mark 9:33-37

-With the Pharisees over healing on the Sabbath: Matthew 12:9-14

-With the Pharisees over driving out demons: Matthew 12:22-25

-With the Pharisees and Sadducees who wanted Him to work miracles to show off His power: Matthew 16:1-4

-With the money changers in the temple: Mark 11:15-18

-With the Sanhedrin and Roman rulers because He refused to deny He was God's Son: Mark 14:60-63; 15:15

4. There are many Biblical examples of how leaders confronted conflict and discipline matters and successfully dealt with them. Study the following references:

-Moses: Numbers 16; Exodus 18:13-26

-King Solomon: I Kings 3:16-28

-Nathan confronts David: II Samuel 12

-Samuel confronts Saul: I Samuel 15

-Nehemiah: Nehemiah 13:23-25

-Church leaders at Jerusalem: Acts 15

-God's discipline of all believers: Hebrews 12:5-7

-Apostle Paul: Galatians 2:11

CHAPTER TEN

TRAINING LEADERS AND FOLLOWERS

OBJECTIVES:

Upon completion of this chapter you will be able to:

- Write the Key Verse from memory.
- Explain the purpose for training leaders and followers.
- Explain why training others is an important responsibility.
- Identify six principles of selection used by Jesus.
- Identify eight principles of training used by Jesus.
- Give a Biblical example of a leadership training model.

KEY VERSE

> **A disciple is not above his teacher, but everyone when he is fully taught will be like his teacher. (Luke 6:40) Revised Standard Version**

INTRODUCTION

Leaders must have followers and followers must have leaders. In an average church, no one is designated to develop leaders and followers, yet the future of the Church depends on them. The training of leaders and followers should begin in childhood preparing youngsters to take their part in the body of Christ. Training should immediately follow conversion at any age.

You have learned that God gives to some believers special gifts of leadership. Others are born with natural abilities to lead. Some people seem to be natural followers. Everyone is called to be both a leader and a follower.

Whether naturally talented or gifted by God, leaders and followers need training. "Each one teach one to reach one" is God's answer to the leadership shortage:

> **And the things that thou has heard of me among many witnesses, the same commit thou to faithful men, who shall be able to teach others also.**
> **(II Timothy 2:2)**

In this chapter, you will learn how to train leaders and followers.

FOLLOWERS

Everyone is a follower. Paul speaks of himself as a follower of Jesus and calls upon the Corinthians to follow him:

> **Be ye followers of me, even as I also am of Christ. (I Corinthians 11:1)**

Similar instructions were given to the Ephesians (Ephesians 5:1; Philippians (Philippians 3:17); and Thessalonians (I Thessalonians 1:6).

Each believer should be trained to be a good follower. Many of us do not want to be followers. We would rather be leaders. But a good leader is first a good follower. A leader is always responsible to someone else, so he is also a follower. We lead successfully by following successfully.

To be a good follower you must obey your leaders and submit to their authority so their work is a joy:

> **Obey them that have the rule over you, and submit yourselves: for they watch for your souls, as they that must give account, that they may do it with joy and not with grief; for that is unprofitable for you.**
> **(Hebrews 13:17)**

Followers should follow their leaders only as long as they follow Christ. When leaders stray from the truth of God's Word, do not follow them.

LEADERS

Not everyone is called to a leadership position in the Church, but each person leads in some way from time to time. For example, a man may not be called to leadership in the Church, but he is the leader in his home.

A believer may not have a spiritual gift of leadership but because of needs in the church may find it necessary to fill a leadership role occasionally. For these reasons, all believers should be trained in leadership.

AN IMPORTANT RESPONSIBILITY

Training others is an important responsibility because...

> **A disciple is not above his teacher, but everyone when he is fully taught will be like his teacher. (Luke 6:40) Revised Standard Version**

The people you train will be like you! You have an important responsibility to set a proper example by your conduct and lifestyle.

THE PURPOSE IN TRAINING

The reason we train leaders and followers is to fulfill the commission given by Jesus:

> **Go ye therefore, and teach all nations, baptizing them in the name of the Father, and of the Son, and of the Holy Ghost;**
>
> **Teaching them to observe all things whatsoever I have commanded you: and, lo, I am with you alway, even unto the end of the world. (Matthew 28:19-20)**

We train leaders and followers for the purpose of going to all nations, teaching the Gospel, baptizing, and then guiding converts on to spiritual maturity through further teaching. People must hear the Gospel in order to respond, repent from sin, and be born again. Such teaching is also called "evangelism":

> **Go ye therefore and teach all nations, baptizing them in the name of the Father, and of the Son, and of the Holy Ghost. (Matthew 28:19)**

New believers are sometimes called "converts." A convert is a believer in Jesus who has been born again by faith and has become part of the Kingdom of God. But a new convert must be trained to be a follower. New converts are to be instructed in all Jesus taught:

> **Teaching them to observe all things whatsoever I have commanded you: and, lo, I am with you alway, even unto the end of the world. (Matthew 28:20)**

The plan of Jesus is that we lead converts on to discipleship. The word "disciple" means a "learner, a pupil, someone who learns by following." A disciple is a follower who is established in the basics of the Christian faith and capable of raising up new converts and discipling them. As he does this, he becomes a leader. As this process is repeated, new followers and leaders are continuously raised up to extend the Gospel of the Kingdom.

CONVERTS, TO FOLLOWERS, TO LEADERS

How do you lead people from being converts to become disciples (followers) and then leaders? You must train them. Winning new converts is important, but only by training them as followers and leaders will they be able to reproduce spiritually.

Jesus demonstrated this as He selected followers and trained them to become leaders. He had only 3½ years of ministry in which to do the work God had given Him. He was able to visit only a few places during this short period of time and reach only a limited number of people

.

To assure completion of His mission, Jesus made training followers and leaders a priority. He knew those He trained would reach multitudes of villages and cities that He would never have opportunity to visit.

PRINCIPLES OF SELECTION

You are just one person with only so much available time, so you cannot train everyone. This means you must select those whom you will train. How will you select those you will train? You could choose on the basis of education, experience, tests, or by trial and error.

But the best way to select is to follow principles Jesus used in selecting His disciples. The record of His selection is given in Matthew 5:1; 10:2-4; Mark 3:13-19; Luke 6:12-16; and Luke 10:1-16. Here are some important principles Jesus followed which you can use in selecting those you will train:

DEPEND ON GOD:

Jesus depended on God. He said:

> **I can of mine own self do nothing... because I seek not mine own will, but the will of the Father which hath sent me. (John 5:30)**

MAKE IT A MATTER OF PRAYER:

Luke 6:12-13 records that Jesus spent the whole night in prayer before selecting His disciples. Pray to God for wisdom to select faithful men and women for training.

TAKE THE INITIATIVE:

Jesus took the initiative to call His disciples. People will not flock to you to become followers or leaders. You must take the initiative to call them.

LOOK AT POTENTIAL, NOT PROBLEMS:

When Jesus selected disciples, He called common men. Some were uneducated and they all had faults and failures. It has been said that if the original 12 disciples were reviewed by a church mission board in the present time, they would be turned down for missionary service.

But Jesus operated on the basis of potential, not problems. He did not choose men and women because of what they were, but because of what they could become. He looked beyond the problems to their potential.

MAKE THE COSTS CLEAR:

When Jesus selected disciples, He made it clear what it cost. A true follower or leader must forsake all:

> **So likewise, whosoever he be of you that forsaketh not all that he hath, he cannot be my disciple. (Luke 14:33)**

He must deny self by taking up the cross:

> **Then said Jesus unto His disciples, If any man will come after me, let him deny himself, and take up his cross, and follow me. (Matthew 16:24)**
>
> **And whosoever doth not bear his cross, and come after me, cannot be my disciple. (Luke 14:27)**

He must follow Jesus:

> **Then said Jesus unto His disciples, If any man will come after me, let him deny himself, and take up his cross, and follow. (Matthew 16:24)**

The Kingdom of God must become his main priority:

> **Therefore take no thought, saying, What shall we eat? or What shall we drink? or, Wherewithal shall we be clothed?...**
>
> **But seek ye first the Kingdom of God, and His righteousness; and all these things shall be added unto you. (Matthew 6:31,33)**

God has promised to supply all your needs if His Kingdom is the priority of your life.

A follower must become a servant to all:

> **The disciple is not above His master, nor the servant above His lord. (Matthew 10:25)**

But it shall not be so among you: but whosoever will be great among you, let him be your minister:

> **And whosoever will be chief among you, let him be your servant;**
>
> **Even as the Son of man came not to be ministered unto, but to minister, and to give His life a ransom for many. (Matthew 20:26-28)**

SELECT THOSE WHO MEET BASIC REQUIREMENTS:

Paul told Timothy to select faithful men and commit to them the things he had been taught. These faithful men were to have the ability to teach others. The basic requirements are faithfulness and the ability to teach others. If a man is not faithful, he will not fulfill his responsibility of spiritual reproduction. If he is faithful but does not know how to teach others, then he will also fail.

Faithfulness involves spiritual maturity. Paul spoke of believers who should have been able to teach others but had not yet matured spiritually. These people are not yet ready for true discipleship. They must be further instructed in the basics of the faith.

Faithful men are not necessarily faultless men. They are believers who are in the process of developing Christ-like qualities in their lives. Even "faithful men" have problems and weaknesses to overcome, as did the original disciples.

The world takes talented men and attempts to give them character. They focus on creating professionals. God said to take "faithful men" of character and He will empower them with spiritual talents and abilities. Faithful men are available to accomplish God's purposes. When Jesus called Simon and Andrew, they "immediately" left their nets. The word "immediately" reveals their availability.

When you select men and women to disciple, they must be available. They must be willing to make discipleship the priority of their lives. Faithful men are motivated by spiritual vision. When Jesus gave Peter and Andrew the vision of catching men and women, it motivated them to leave their nets.

Faithful men have a hunger for the Word of God, as did Christ's disciples. Their "hearts burned within them" as He shared the Scriptures (Luke 24:32,45). They were willing and eager to be taught. Faithful men are marked by a love for God and man. They take seriously the first and second greatest commands:

And thou shalt love the Lord thy God with all thy heart, and with all thy soul, and with all thy mind, and with all thy strength: this is the first commandment.

And the second is like, namely this, Thou shalt love thy neighbor as thyself. There is none other commandment greater than these. (Mark 12:30-31)

PRINCIPLES OF TRAINING

After selecting His disciples, Jesus demonstrated eight important principles in training them:

1. ASSOCIATION:

When Jesus called His disciples, He called them to "be with Him." He shared His life intimately with His disciples. He spent time with them in both formal ministry situations and informal circumstances. You cannot train followers and leaders through committee meetings or Sunday worship services alone. There must be close association with those whom you train. You must share your life with them. You must come to know them, their problems, their spiritual level, etc.

2. CONSECRATION:

Out of association with Jesus, consecration developed. Jesus called His disciples to consecrate to a Person, not a denomination or organization. Such consecration to God called for absolute obedience to His Word and purposes. (See John 4:34; 5:30; 15:10; 17:4; and Luke 22:42).

3. VISION:

Jesus motivated His followers by giving them spiritual vision. He called them to a task greater than the routine of everyday living. He called them to be fishers of men (Matthew 4:19). He gave them a vision of worldwide spiritual harvest (John 4:35). He challenged them with the revelation of the Kingdom of God (Matthew 13).

Without vision, people perish (Proverbs 29:18). They have no direction and no motivation. As you train others you must communicate spiritual vision to motivate the mission. The vision is worldwide conquest with the Gospel of the Kingdom. Never be distracted by a lesser cause.

4. INSTRUCTION:

Jesus spent a great part of His time teaching His disciples. His instruction always related to the vision He had given them. If you are to train disciples following the methods of Jesus, then you must teach what Jesus taught. This is part of the command of the Great Commission (Matthew 28:20).

Emphasis should be on the teachings of Jesus and what was revealed as these teachings were put into practice in the first Church. This means the focus of teaching should be on the Gospels and the Epistles of the New Testament. (Harvestime International Institute curriculum provides such training. Harvestime also offers a course entitled *"Teaching Tactics"* which trains you to teach using the methods of Jesus.)

As you teach what Jesus taught, you teach the entire revelation of God's Word because it is based on the Old Testament. Jesus said:

> **...These are the words which I spake unto you, while I was yet with you, that all things must be fulfilled, which were written in the law of Moses, and in the prophets, and in the psalms concerning me...**
>
> **...Thus it is written, and thus it behooved Christ to suffer, and to rise from the dead the third day:**
>
> **And that repentance and remission of sins should be preached in His name among all nations, beginning at Jerusalem. (Luke 24:44,46-47)**

5. DEMONSTRATION:

Jesus did not teach through verbal instruction alone. He demonstrated what He taught. Jesus taught healing and demonstrated it by healing the sick. He taught the authority of the believer over Satan and demonstrated it by casting out demons. He taught concern for the poor and illustrated it by feeding the multitudes.

The disciples were not only students, they were eye witnesses to the demonstration of God's power. They later said they were teaching "That which we have seen and heard" as "eye witnesses" (I John 1:1).

Jesus taught by example. He demonstrated what He said by how He lived and ministered. He said:

> **For I gave you an example that you also should do as I did to you. (John 13:15)**

The demonstration of God's power makes people listen to your message:

> **And the people with one accord gave heed unto those things which Philip spake, hearing and seeing the miracles which he did. (Acts 8:6)**

Paul spoke not only of the truth of the Gospel (Galatians 2:5) but of the power of the Gospel (Romans 1:16). He declared and demonstrated the Gospel (I Corinthians 2:1,4). (Harvestime International Institute has a course entitled *"Power Principles"* devoted to this subject).

6. PARTICIPATION:

Mere knowledge is not enough. To be effective, knowledge must be applied. There comes a time for action. The disciples not only listened to the teachings of Jesus and observed the demonstrations, they also participated. Teaching a subject is not enough to assure learning.

Teaching alone is like trying to learn to do surgery by reading a book.

Disciples must have actual experience in what they are learning. They must gain experience in how to share the Gospel, how to pray for the sick, how to cast out demons, etc. Jesus provided such opportunities for His disciples. Read Mark 6:7-13 and Luke 9:1-6. Jesus sent His disciples out to experience what they had been taught. Those you train become doers of the Word and not hearers only.

7. SUPERVISION:

When the disciples of Jesus returned from their ministry trip, Jesus evaluated their efforts (Luke 9:10). Throughout the entire training process Jesus supervised His disciples. They were not left alone in their struggles. He was there to correct, rebuke, and encourage them.

You cannot assume that the work will be done merely because you have shown a willing worker how to do it and sent him out with glowing expectations. You must supervise. As the worker faces frustration and obstacles, you must teach him how to meet these challenges.

Supervision is sometimes called "follow-up." Paul supervised or "followed-up" on his disciples:

> **And after he had spent some time there, he departed and went over all the country of Galatia, and Phyrgia in order, strengthening all the disciples. (Acts 18:23)**
>
> **Confirming the souls of the disciples, and exhorting them to continue in the faith, and that we must through much tribulation enter into the Kingdom of God. (Acts 14:22)**

8. DELEGATION:

The final stage of the discipleship process was when Jesus delegated His followers to become disciple-makers themselves. He gave them the task of spiritual multiplication throughout the nations of the world.

THE EXAMPLE OF EPHESUS

Read Acts 19:1-20 in your Bible. This chapter describes the ministry of the Apostle Paul at a city named Ephesus. When Paul first arrived in Ephesus, he sought out believers who lived there. These men and women had already accepted the Gospel and become followers of Jesus (Acts 19:1) but they needed further training in order to minister effectively in their city.

Paul taught them through experience. The first thing he did was lead them into a new spiritual experience which was the baptism of the Holy Ghost (Acts 19:2-8). Paul taught them through demonstration. They witnessed many great miracles done in the name of the Lord (Acts 19:11-

12). Those who were not true followers of Jesus were exposed and repented (Acts 19:13-17). New converts were won to the Lord Jesus Christ (Acts 19:17-20).

When opposition to the Gospel arose from traditional leaders, Paul established a training center at Ephesus:

> **But when divers were hardened, and believed not, but spake evil of that way before the multitude, he (Paul) departed from them, and separated the disciples, disputing daily in the school of one Tyrannus. (Acts 19:9)**

Ephesus is an excellent example of a model program of leadership training. Paul did not remove students from their native environment to receive training. He trained them in an environment which was natural to them. They remained in their own community and learned in their own language.

The center Paul established offered a two-year training course for disciples. The purpose of the school was to multiply disciples who would spread the Gospel message:

> **And this continued by the space of two years; so that all they which dwelt in Asia heard the word of the Lord Jesus Christ, both Jews and Greeks. (Acts 19:10)**

This training center knew no cultural lines. Students ministered to both Jews and Gentiles (other non-Jewish nations of the world). The school had no geographic boundaries. The students not only ministered in their own city of Ephesus, they reached the entire continent of Asia.

The Ephesus example is a good model of training because those trained taught others...

> **...So that all they which dwelt in Asia heard the word of the Lord Jesus Christ, both Jews and Greeks. (Acts 19:10)**
>
> **So mightily grew the Word of God and prevailed. (Acts 19:20)**

The Ephesus school trained disciples and equipped them for the work of the ministry. The purpose was to spread the Gospel geographically (throughout all Asia) and culturally (to both Jews and Gentiles). New converts were then trained as disciples in a continued process of multiplication.

STARTING A TRAINING CENTER

The need for training centers similar to the Ephesus model exists today. As converts multiply, it is important that they be trained as followers and leaders who are challenged with their responsibility of reaching the world with the Gospel.

The training center at Ephesus did not replace the church. Believers continued to meet in the synagogue, which was one gathering place of the early church. Believers also continued to meet in churches in their homes. The Ephesus school was an extension of the church and not a replacement for it. The purpose of such a training program is not to replace any existing institution actively spreading the Gospel.

If you are interested in starting a training center similar to the Ephesus model, instructions for doing this are provided in the Harvestime International Institute course entitled *"Multiplication Methodologies."* It explains how to select a location, set a budget, recruit students, select teachers and curriculum, and publicize and conduct sessions.

SELF-TEST

1. Write the Key Verse from memory.

____

____

2. Why is training others an important responsibility?

____

3. What is the purpose of training leaders and followers?

____

4. List six principles of selection discussed in the study of Jesus and His disciples.

_______________________ _______________________

_______________________ _______________________

_______________________ _______________________

5. List eight principles of training discussed in the study of Jesus and His disciples.

_______________________ _______________________

_______________________ _______________________

_______________________ _______________________

_______________________ _______________________

6. What New Testament example was given as a model of leadership training?

____

(Answers to tests are provided at the conclusion of the final chapter in this manual.)

FOR FURTHER STUDY

1. Followers become leaders:

   -Joshua, who was a follower of Moses, became a leader: Numbers 27:18; Deuteronomy 3:28

   -Elisha, who was a follower of Elijah, became a leader: II Kings 2

2. Jesus trained followers who became leaders. The repeated call of Jesus Christ was a call to follow. The words "follow," "follow me," and "come after me" are used by Jesus more than 20 times. They are addressed to:

-Simon and Andrew:	Matthew 4:19; Mark 1:17
-James and John:	Matthew 4:21; Mark 1:20 (implied)
-Matthew:	Matthew 9:9; Mark 2:14; Luke 5:27
-Philip:	John 1:43
-Peter:	John 21:19,22
-The rich young ruler:	Matthew 19:21; Mark 10:21; Luke 18:22
-Another of His disciples:	Matthew 8:22
-Any man:	Matthew 16:24; Mark 8:34; Luke 9:23; John 12:26

3. Read about the training of leaders in Old Testament times in I Samuel 19:18-20 and II Kings 2:1; 4:38; 6:1.

4. Here are the five main obstacles you must overcome in training followers and leaders:

   1. Fear of man.
   2. Laziness.
   3. Resistance to change.
   4. Conflicting priorities.
   5. Ignorance (people must be trained in how to share the Gospel and perform specific tasks of ministry).

5. Harvestime International Institute courses can assist you in training both followers and leaders. Write today for a complete listing of the courses offered.

6. Here are guidelines for conducting a training session:

Be Prepared:

Each teacher should be thoroughly acquainted with the subject matter he is to teach. He should prepare through prayer. He should have proper supplies and materials ready for each class session.

Each teacher should have specific objectives for each lesson. If you are using Harvestime International Institute materials, objectives are listed at the beginning of each chapter.

Be sure the classrooms are ready for the students.

Be Punctual:

Start and conclude class sessions on time. (Unless the Holy Spirit leads otherwise.)

Pray:

Open and close class sessions in prayer.

Review And Summarize:

Start each class session with a brief review of what was taught in the last class session. Close each class with a summary of the lesson taught in that session.

Use Various Teaching Methods:

The Harvestime International Institute course entitled *"Teaching Tactics"* trains you to teach using the methods of Jesus.

Be Open To The Holy Spirit:

Being open to the moving of the Holy Spirit is more important than completing the lesson or following a planned format.

Demonstrate:

Demonstrate what is being taught. For example, if you are teaching on healing, pray for those present who are sick. When teaching on the baptism of the Holy Spirit, lead people to experience it.

Plan Learning Experiences:

Give study assignments for students to complete between class sessions. Provide opportunities for them to put into practice what they are learning by practical ministry in their church and community.

7. Here are some questions for you to consider:

-Is your example before others leading them to live for God? List three ways you can tell.

-Do others have the opportunity to be with you in order to observe your example or do you remain aloof from people? List three ways you regularly open yourself up to others.

-Do you really believe the example of your life should be followed by others? Why or why not? How can you improve your example?

-Are you violating a known principle of God's Word in the exercise of your leadership? In what way? How can you correct this?

-Can you name someone you have trained to help you?

CHAPTER ELEVEN

FACING FAILURE

OBJECTIVES;

Upon completion of this chapter you will be able to:

- Write the Key Verse from memory.
- Identify three basic causes for failure.
- Identify Biblical leaders who triumphed over failure.
- Identify Biblical leaders whose lives ended in failure.
- List Biblical guidelines for turning failure to success.

KEY VERSE;

A just man falleth seven times, and riseth up again. (Proverbs 24:16)

INTRODUCTION

This lesson is one of the most important ones in this course on *"Biblical Management Principles."* It deals with failure. God has perfect plans, but He works through imperfect leaders to accomplish His plans. Because you are imperfect, you must understand the reasons for failure and know what to do when you fail.

In this lesson you will learn the basic causes of failure. You will study examples of leaders whose lives ended in failure and those who turned failure into success. You will also be given Biblical guidelines for facing failure and turning it to success.

WHAT CAUSES FAILURE?

There are three basic reasons for failure:

1. FAILURE IN RELATIONSHIP:

Many leaders fail because they have an improper relationship with God. They may not have developed the proper spiritual foundations listed in Hebrews 6:1-3. When they try to build a work for God on a poor spiritual foundation, it collapses.

Some leaders get so busy doing "God's work" that they neglect prayer, Bible study, fasting, and seeking the Lord and His will. Others lose their first intense love of the Lord Jesus Christ. Instead of God and His Kingdom being the priority, cares and riches of the world, making money, or pleasing people begin to take first place in their lives.

King Uzziah is an example of a leader who failed because of his own relationship with God. King Uzziah started well. He sought the Lord (II Chronicles 26:6-8). He did well in battles against Israel's enemies (II Chronicles 26:6-8). But when King Uzziah became well known and prideful, he began to "act corruptly," was unfaithful to God, and no longer sought the Lord (II Chronicles 26:16).

To be a leader, you must have close fellowship with God. Many leaders who have failed discover that their problem began with a failure in their own personal relationship with God.

2. FAILURE BY COMMISSION:

"Failure by commission" means failure caused by your own sinful actions. Sins of "commission" include every wrong action, word, attitude or motive. Such acts or sins of "commission" result in failure.

3. FAILURE BY OMISSION:

"Failure by omission" means failure caused by what you do not do. When you sin by "omission," you fail to do what you should do. The Bible says:

> **For to him that knoweth to do right and doeth it not it is sin. (James 4:17)**

Sins of "omission" are things the Word of God says you should do but which you fail to do. Jesus rebuked the religious leaders of His time for such "omissions." He said...

> **Woe unto you, scribes and Pharisees, hypocrites! for ye pay tithe of mint and anise and cummin, and have omitted the weightier matters of the law, judgment, mercy, and faith; these ought ye to have done, and not leave the other undone. (Matthew 23:23)**

LEADERS WHO TRIUMPHED OVER THEIR FAILURES

The Bible contains many examples of great men who at some point in their lives failed as leaders:

Abraham: He lied about Sarah being his wife for fear he would be killed and his wife taken from him. Yet he is called a man of faith and the "friend of God."

Moses: In anger he struck the rock and called forth water instead of speaking to the rock as God directed. Yet the Bible says there has never been another prophet as great as Moses.

King David: He committed adultery with another man's wife, then had the man killed to try to cover his sin. Yet he was a great king and is called "a man after God's own heart."

Jonah: He went the opposite direction when God called him to preach in Ninevah. Later he preached the greatest revival in history. The whole city repented.

Joshua: This man was a great military commander who assumed leadership of the nation of Israel after the death of Moses. One of the challenges God gave Joshua was to lead Israel to claim their promised land. But at one point Joshua was so discouraged that he longed to be back on the other side of Jordan in the wilderness. At another time he was deceived by the Gibeonites. Yet this man went on to conquer the land promised by God.

The Prophet Elijah: A wicked queen named Jezebel sent a messenger to the prophet Elijah informing him she was planning to kill him. Elijah...

> **...went a day's journey into the wilderness and came and sat down under a juniper tree: and he requested for himself that he might die; and said, It is enough; now, O Lord, take away my life; for I am not better than my fathers. (I Kings 19:4)**

Here was the great man of God who had healed the sick, raised the dead, and controlled elements of nature in the name of the Lord. Now he was hiding, fearful, despondent, and requesting to die. Yet Elijah returned to demonstrate God's power before the entire nation of Israel at Mt. Carmel.

Peter: This man denied Jesus, but later became a great leader in the early church.

The Apostle Paul: The Apostle Paul also faced failure. He wrote once that due to experiences in Asia he was "pressed out of measure" and "despaired even of life" (II Corinthians 1:8). He expressed times when he was troubled, perplexed, persecuted, and cast down (II Corinthians 4:8-ll). He said he had fears and troubles (II Corinthians 7:5-6). But the Apostle Paul successfully spread the Gospel to the Gentiles, raising up great churches and leaders throughout the nations of the world.

LEADERS WHOSE FAILURES ENDED IN DEFEAT

The Bible also contains many examples of leaders whose lives ended in failure and defeat:

Samson: Who was a great judge of Israel and had great physical strength given him from God. He began to deliver Israel from the Philistine enemy. Through involvement with a heathen woman, Samson was taken captive and died while yet a prisoner of the enemy.

Uzziah: He became a king when he was 16 years old and as long as he did what was right in the sight of the Lord, he prospered. Uzziah sinned by entering the temple and performing duties which only the priests were permitted to do. God smote him with leprosy and he died.

Saul: Saul was the first king of Israel, adored by the people, and a man upon whom the Spirit of God rested. Because of disobedience, Saul was rejected by God and another king was selected to complete his task. Saul's life ended in failure, disgrace, and suicide.

Eli: He was originally a great priest in the house of the Lord. Because of disobedience, Eli and his sons died in disgrace.

Judas: Judas was a disciple of Jesus during His earthly ministry. He witnessed the great miracles of Jesus and heard His teachings. Yet he betrayed Jesus and ended his own life by suicide.

WHAT MADE THE DIFFERENCE?

Some of these leaders recovered from their failures and went on to be great men of God. Others never changed. Their lives ended in defeat. What made the difference?

To answer this question, let us examine in more detail the lives of two great leaders of the nation of Israel, the kings David and Saul. First, read the story of David's failure in II Samuel chapters 11-12. Then read the story of Saul's failure in I Samuel chapter 15.

In our human reasoning, David's failure seems so much greater than that of Saul. Saul simply brought back some oxen as spoil from battle when God had directed him not to do so. David committed adultery with another man's wife. When it was discovered she was pregnant, he had her husband killed to try to cover the sin. Saul was rejected by God as king, yet David remained on the throne and was called "a man after God's own heart."

Why did one man's life end in failure while the other went on to future successes? The answer is one word: Repentance. When the prophet Samuel confronted Saul with his sin, Saul said...

> **...I have sinned: for I have transgressed the commandment of the Lord, and thy words: because I feared the people, and obeyed their voice.**
> **Then he said, I have sinned; yet honor me now, I pray thee, before the elders of my people and before Israel, and turn again with me, that I worship the Lord thy God. (I Samuel 15:24 and 30)**

Saul was caught in his sin and he admitted it. He was sorry, but only for being caught. Being sorry for sin is not enough. That sorrow must lead to repentance:

For godly sorrow worketh repentance to salvation not to be repented of: but the sorrow of the world worketh death. (II Corinthians 7:10)

Saul admitted he had failed, but he blamed his failure on other people. He wanted Samuel to honor him before the leaders of the people so he would not be disgraced. He wanted Samuel to worship God with him to show to the people he was still a spiritual man.

Saul never confessed his sin to God, repented, and asked forgiveness. He refused to accept personal responsibility for his actions. He offered God worship when God wanted repentance. Saul was more concerned about his reputation among the people than his relationship to God. He saw the Kingdom not as God's Kingdom, but as a way to build his own empire.

Because of this, Samuel told Saul:

...The Lord hath rent the kingdom of Israel from thee this day, and hath given it to a neighbor of thine, that is better than thou. (I Samuel 15:28)

The kingdom was taken from Saul and given to David.

When the prophet Nathan confronted David about his sin, David immediately acknowledged:

I have sinned against the Lord. (II Samuel 12:13)

He did not try to blame others. He did not blame Bathsheba. He admitted his failure and humbly repented before God. David's great prayer of repentance is recorded in Psalms 51. Read this entire Psalm in your Bible. David acknowledged his sin and asked forgiveness:

For I acknowledge my transgressions: and my sin is ever before me.

**Against thee, thee only have I sinned and done this evil in thy sight...
Create in me a clean heart O God; and renew a right spirit within me.
(Psalms 51:3,4,10)**

When confronted with failure, David repented and changed direction. Saul did not. He strayed farther from the will of God and his life ended in failure, defeat, and suicide.

WHEN YOU FAIL

When you fail there are Biblical guidelines which, if you follow them, can turn failure into success. To study these guidelines we will use the example of Jonah. Read the book of Jonah (four chapters) in your Bible before proceeding with this lesson.

Jonah was commanded by the Lord to go and preach repentance to the sinful nation of Nineveh. Instead of obeying God's voice, he headed the opposite direction. Jonah took the following steps to correct his failure. These are steps to take when you experience failure:

REVEALING:

When you fail, ask God to reveal the cause of that failure. Be assured: God has ways of letting you know when you have failed. A great storm at sea revealed Jonah was out of the will of God. Jonah admitted his guilt after this revelation (Jonah 1:12). As long as you do not acknowledge your failure you will remain a failure:

> **He that covereth his sins shall not prosper; but whoso confesseth and forsaketh them shall have mercy. (Proverbs 28:13)**

> **If we say that we have no sin, we deceive ourselves, and the truth is not in us. (I John 1:8)**

Do not let any excuse prevent you from admitting failure. Here are some common ones:

-"People will lose confidence in me."
-"If I admit failure it is admitting I was wrong."
-"I already failed. I might as well give up."
-"It's too late."
-"I am a bad example, so I should just quit."
-"I am too far out of God's will to get things right."

It is not necessary to reveal your failure publicly unless it has affected the lives of others and you must seek their forgiveness. But you must always admit your failure to yourself and to God. This is the first step to change failure to success: The sin must be revealed. You must confront it.

REPENTING:

After the cause of your failure is revealed, you must repent:

> **If we confess our sins, He is faithful and just to forgive us our sins, and to cleanse us from all unrighteousness. (I John 1:9)**

Jonah's great prayer of repentance is recorded in Jonah chapter 2. Jonah acknowledged his sin before God, repented, and asked forgiveness. When you fail, come before the Lord in repentance. Ask God to forgive you for your failure. Be sure to forgive yourself, too!

RETURNING:

Through prayer, the written Word of God, and the guidance of the Holy Spirit, God will reveal to you the point at which your failure began. You must then return to that point and reverse your direction.

In the case of Jonah, he realized his failure began when he went the opposite direction from Nineveh. He had to return to this point of failure and reverse his direction. True repentance involves a change in direction. When you return to a point of failure you go back to where you first sinned and correct your error. This is done by...

RESTORING:

In the case of Jonah, when he recognized his failure began by heading the opposite direction from Nineveh, he reversed directions. He went towards Nineveh. He corrected his failure (Jonah 3:3). He did what he could to make things right. This is called "restoring."

Sometimes you can do nothing to correct your failure except repent. In the example of David which we discussed, he could do nothing about his sin with Bathsheba after it was committed. The mistake was already made. The adultery was committed and her husband was dead. There was nothing he could do to correct it except repent.

But in situations where you can return to the point of failure and make restitution, you must do so. You may have to apologize to someone. You may have to return something you have stolen or admit you told a lie. These are all examples of restoration.

You also need time to restore yourself and rebuild your spiritual strength after failure. You may need to temporarily step down from ministry responsibilities. You will definitely need time alone with God.

Here are some ways to restore your spiritual strength:

-Study God's Word.

-Spend time in prayer and fasting.

-Review the basic causes for failure (given in this lesson) so you will be able to avoid future failures. Ask God to reveal and help you correct any problem areas in your life.

-Review strategies of spiritual warfare to help you wage more effective warfare next time. (See the Harvestime International Institute course entitled *"Spiritual Strategies: A Manual of Spiritual Warfare."*)

-Rest physically. Man is body, soul, and spirit. When your physical body is exhausted, Satan can take advantage and affect your soul and spirit and cause you to fail.

ON TO SUCCESS!

After you have taken these steps, put your failure behind you and go on to success. Jonah put his failure behind Him. The Lord spoke unto him a second time and said, "Arise, and go to Ninevah" (Jonah 3:1-2). This time he quickly obeyed. In Ninevah, Jonah led one of the greatest revivals in history. The whole city repented. By following the steps of revealing, repenting, returning, and restoring, his failure was turned to success.

The Bible contains many stories of men like Jonah. These men failed but admitted their failure and asked forgiveness of God. When they did, God never failed to forgive and provide new direction. This is the Biblical pattern for turning failure into success.

God can do the same for you! He is not looking at your past failures. He is not looking at you as you are today. He is seeing the man or woman...the leader you can be if you only walk in obedience to Him.

LEARNING FROM FAILURE

Paul wrote:

> **For we would not, brethren, have you ignorant of our trouble which came to us in Asia, that we were pressed out of measure, above strength, insomuch that we despaired even of life.**
>
> **But we had the sentence of death in ourselves, that we should not trust in ourselves, but in the God which raiseth the dead;**
>
> **Who delivered us from so great a death, and doth deliver, in whom we trust that He will yet deliver us. (II Corinthians 1:8-10)**

Paul explained that problems in Asia taught him an important lesson..."we should not trust in ourselves, but in God." This is a great lesson to learn from failure. You cannot trust in yourself. Your power, your authority, your success as a leader is assured only in Christ Jesus. Paul looked beyond the natural world to see the spiritual benefits of problems, temptations, trials, and failures:

> **For which cause we faint not: but though our outward man perish, yet the inward man is renewed day by day.**
>
> **For our light affliction, which is but for a moment, worketh for us a far more exceeding and eternal weight of glory;**

While we look not at the things which are seen, but at the things, which are not seen: for the things which are seen are temporal; but the things which are not seen are eternal. (II Corinthians 4:16-18)

Paul had learned that even though the outward man perished, the inward man was being renewed. Instead of giving up, Paul learned from failure and went on to success. In II Corinthians 1:10 he indicated that God...

"Delivered"	(In the past)
"Does deliver"	(In the present)
"Will yet deliver"	(In the future)

...us from all of our problems, trials, temptations, and failures. He said we were...

Troubled....BUT NOT DISTRESSED.
Perplexed...BUT NOT IN DESPAIR.
Persecuted...BUT NOT FORSAKEN.
Cast down...BUT NOT DESTROYED!
(II Corinthians 4:8-9)

In spite of all the perplexities, persecution, trouble, and despair, Paul was able to say in the closing days of his life:

I have fought a good fight, I have finished my course, I have kept the faith. (II Timothy 4:7)

SELF-TEST

1. Write the Key Verse from memory.

____

____

2. List three Biblical examples of great leaders who triumphed over their failures.

____

____

____

3. Identify three Biblical examples of men whose lives ended in failure.

____

____

____

4. List Biblical guidelines for turning failure to success:

R____________________ R____________________

R____________________ R____________________

5. What are three basic causes of failure?

____

____

____

(Answers to tests are provided at the conclusion of the final chapter in this manual.)

FOR FURTHER STUDY

1. In Luke 15:11-32 Jesus told the story of a young man who left his father and went to live in a strange country. Study this story carefully, especially the portion which tells of the son's return to the house of his father. You will discover he followed the same guidelines for correcting failure which were discussed in this chapter.

2. Study the following list of Biblical examples of leaders who failed at some point in their lives. Which ones corrected their failures? How did they turn their failures into success? Which ones did not correct their failures? What was the result? You can add other examples to this list from your own study of God's Word.

-Abraham:	Genesis 20-21
-Moses:	Book Of Exodus; Acts 7:20-44
-Aaron:	Exodus 32
-Balaam:	Numbers 22
-Uzziah:	II Chronicles 26
-Samson:	Judges 13-16
-David:	II Samuel 11-12; Psalms 51
-Saul:	I Samuel 8-15
-Jonah:	The book of Jonah
-Peter:	Matthew, Mark, Luke, John, Acts
-John Mark:	Acts 12:12,25; 15:39; II Timothy 4:11
-Demas:	II Timothy 4:9

3. You learned in this lesson that there are three basic reasons for failure which include:

   -Failure in personal relationship with God (wrong spiritual foundation, lack of prayer, Bible study).
   -Sins of commission (any violation of God's Word).
   -Sins of omission (not doing what should be done).

   Here is a list of some results of these basic failures. Can you think of other results to add to this list?

   -Discouragement.
   -Emulations (imitating the ministry of others).
   -Lack of vision.
   -Lack of training.
   -Unwilling to pay the price.
   -Lack of commitment.
   -Wrong priorities.

-Immorality.
-Greed, riches, wrong use of funds, love of money.
-Pride.
-Jealousy.
-Mistreating followers.
-Lack of communication to followers.
-Fear of men and respect of persons.
-Popularity.
-Inconsistency.
-Lack of self-evaluation.
-Comparing self to others.
-Compromise.
-Ambition.
-Inability to delegate to others (tries to do it all himself).
-Listens to and obeys man instead of God; swayed by popular opinion.
-Unbelief.
-Inability to lead like a servant and shepherd.
-Not meeting Biblical qualifications for leadership positions.
-Lack of a clear call to leadership.
-Lack of knowledge and application of principles of spiritual warfare.
-Lack of knowledge and application of Biblical principles of success.
-Inability to hear God's voice and discern His will which results in wrong decisions.
-Lack of spiritual power.
-Lack of planning.
-Improper management of spiritual resources.
-Spiritual unfruitfulness.
-Root of bitterness.
-Laziness and slothfulness.
-Love of the world.
-Lack of anointing.

4. Pride is one of the greatest reasons for failure. It was what caused the first sin of mankind. Satan appealed to pride when he said, "You shall be as God." Here are some symptoms of pride:

-Overly conscious of one's importance: Psalms 101:5
-Having "all the answers": Proverbs 3:7
-A proud look: Proverbs 6:17
-More than frequent use of "I" or "my": Isaiah 14:14-15
-Overly conscious of one's good looks: Isaiah 28:1
-Delight in ordering people around: Matthew 20:26-27
-Loving titles: Matthew 23:6-11
-Crediting oneself with work done for God: Acts 12:21-23

-Doing things with the wrong motivation: Romans 8:6
-Scrambling for a seat at the head of the table or line: Mark 12:38-39
-Overly conscious of one's intellect: I Corinthians 3:20
-Over-exhilaration at being around important people: I Corinthians 4:6-7
-Self-commendation: II Corinthians 10:12-13
-Crediting self with work done by others: II Corinthians 10:15
-Having little concern for others: Philippians 2:2-4
-Being anxious about questions and semantics: I Timothy 6:4
-Boasting of what one plans to do: James 4:16
-Ignoring the advice of older, spiritual people: I Peter 5:5-6
-Being irritatingly independent: Ephesians 5:21
-Worrying instead of casting all care upon God: I Peter 5:6-7
-Loving rewards, recognition, position, and compensation: I John 2:15-16

5. Jesus prayed that we would be kept from failure. Read his prayer in John 18:15 and 20.

6. From Matthew 23, make a list of ten positive commandments for Christian leaders. Every failure of the Pharisees can be reversed to give these positive guidelines.

7. The Book of Proverbs contains many warnings of things that result in failure. Read one chapter each day and you can read the book through once each month. Mark in your Bible the things that result in failure and avoid them. (You may want to do this in other books of the Bible also.)

8. The Appendix of this course explains how to study the lives of leaders whose stories are told in the Bible. Study some of the leaders who failed. Make a list of the things which caused their failures.

9. The books of I and II Timothy and Titus were written to young men in leadership positions in ministry. Study these books carefully and list the things which the Apostle Paul told these men to avoid.

CHAPTER TWELVE

SUCCESS PRINCIPLES

OBJECTIVES:

Upon completion of this chapter you will be able to:

- Write the Key Verse from memory.
- Define success.
- Explain how success in God's Kingdom differs from that of the world.
- Summarize basic principles of success.
- Do further study on Biblical principles of success.

KEY VERSE:

> **This book of the law shall not depart out of thy mouth; but thou shalt meditate therein day and night, that thou mayest observe to do according to all that is written therein; for then thou shalt make thy way prosperous, and then thou shalt have good success. (Joshua 1:8)**

INTRODUCTION

Successful people are often asked, "What is the secret of your success?" Those in the world system often list education, position, ambition, talent, power, and money as secrets of success. Many books have been written on the subject, but the true principles of success are revealed in the Bible. In this lesson you will learn Biblical principles of success.

It is assumed that you have already laid the foundations of faith identified in Hebrews 6:1-3. A proper spiritual foundation is necessary in order to apply Biblical success principles in your life and ministry.

WHAT IS SUCCESS?

In God's Kingdom success is "the maximum use of one's gifts and abilities within the range of responsibilities given by God." You are successful when you properly use your spiritual resources for the work of God.

Success in God's Kingdom differs from worldly standards of success. The world views success materially. God views it spiritually. In God's Kingdom there is a different standard that defines success. The world sets its own standard. The standard set by God is called "faithfulness."

There is a different basis of success. The basis of success in the world is changing and temporal. In God's Kingdom, the basis of success is stable and eternal because it is based on revealed truth. There are different motives for success. In the world, people are motivated by greed, pride, and the desire for fame. Believers are motivated to succeed for God's glory.

There is a different model of success in God's Kingdom. The world looks to rich and powerful men. Our model is the Lord Jesus Christ. There is a different goal of success. Money, power and position are stressed as worldly goals. The goal in God's Kingdom is Christlikeness.

Success in God's Kingdom emphasizes giving instead of getting, serving instead of position, humbleness instead of pride, weakness instead of power. The world views success in terms of what you are doing. God views it in terms of what you are. Excellence of character is stressed rather than excellence of achievement.

In God's Kingdom, success is not measured by what you are. It is measured by what you are compared to what you could be. Success is not measured by what you do for God. It is measured by what you do compared to what you could be doing.

SECRETS OF SUCCESS

God wants you to be successful in ministry. He wants you to accomplish the purpose and plans He has for you. Spiritual "secrets of success" are not really secret. They are openly declared in God's Word. They are only "secret" because people refuse to seek and find them.

We cannot cover every principle of success in God's Word because there are so many. The "For Further Study" section of this lesson provides guidelines for continued study of other Biblical principles. But here are some very important basic principles:

HAVE A PROPER HEART ATTITUDE:

Success begins with the hidden man of the heart:

> **...For the Lord seeth not as man seeth; for man looketh on the outward appearance, but the Lord looketh on the heart. (I Samuel 16:7)**

A proper heart attitude includes love, humility, obedience, a serving spirit, and true holiness.

KNOW THE SOURCE OF SUCCESS:

It is not what you know, but who you know that makes you successful. Relationship is based on who you know, not what you know. All of life is based on relationship. Who you know (Jesus) not what you know gets you to Heaven.

Knowing the Lord results in success:

> **Thus saith the Lord, let not the wise man glory in His wisdom, neither let the mighty man glory in his might, let not the rich man glory in his riches. But let him that glorieth glory in this, that he understandeth and knoweth me, that I am the Lord which exercise loving kindness, judgment, and righteousness in the earth... (Jeremiah 9:23-24)**

> **The people that know their God shall be strong and do exploits, and they that understand among the people shall instruct many. (Daniel 11:32-33)**

SEEK THE LORD:

Seeking the Lord means waiting on Him by inquiring of Him, praying, and studying the Word in order to know Him and do His will. The benefits of seeking the Lord were proven by a godly king of Judah called Hezekiah. He sought God and this is the reason for his success:

> **And thus did Hezekiah throughout all Judah, and wrought that which was good and right and truth before the Lord his God.**

> **And in every work that he began in the service of the house of God, and in the law, and in the commandments, to seek His God, he did it with all his heart, and prospered. (II Chronicles 31:20-21)**

It is also said of a king named Uzziah:

> **...And as long as he sought the Lord, God made him to prosper. (II Chronicles 26:5)**

It is important to seek the Lord because God desires to reveal His plans and purposes to leaders (see Amos 3:7.)

MEDITATE ON THE WORD:

Success is promised to those who meditate on the Word of God. The Lord told Joshua:

> **This book of the law shall not depart out of thy mouth; but thou shalt meditate therein day and night, that thou mayest observe to do according to all that is written therein; for then thou shalt make thy way prosperous, and then thou shalt have good success. (Joshua 1:8)**

"Meditate" means "to think about, dwell on, recall, and study in detail." One who meditates believes God has spoken to man, that the Bible is a record of what He has said, and that God's Word is true.

OBEY THE WORD:

It is not just meditation that results in success, it is also obedience to the Word...

> **...that thou mayest observe to do according to all that is written therein; for then thou shalt make thy way prosperous, and then thou shalt have good success. (Joshua 1:8)**

Before Solomon became the King of Israel, David gave him this counsel:

> **Now, my son, the Lord be with thee; and prosper thee, and build the house of the Lord thy God, as He hath said of thee.**
>
> **Only the Lord give thee wisdom and understanding and give thee charge concerning Israel, that thou mayest keep the law of the Lord thy God. (I Chronicles 22:11-12)**

Every commandment in God's Word is important. Keeping these commandments will make you successful.

Not only must you personally meditate on and obey the Word of God, you must elevate it to its proper place of authority before the people you lead. Read how Nehemiah restored the authority of God's Word in Nehemiah 8:1-8. The reforms Nehemiah made would not have lasted apart from the authority of God's Word. A ministry based on the authority of the Word will always succeed.

BE CALLED OF GOD:

You learned previously in this course of the importance of being called of God. You will not be successful unless you know and minister in the specific calling of God, using the spiritual gifts which He has given you.

EXPERIENCE THE PRESENCE OF GOD:

It is the presence of God that prospers ministry:

> **And the Lord was with Joseph, and he was a prosperous man; and he was in the house of his master the Egyptian.**
>
> **And his master saw that the Lord was with him, and that the Lord made all that he did to prosper in his hand. (Genesis 39:2-3)**

God can only be "with you" when you are walking in fellowship with Him, ministering in your specific calling, and living a holy life.

HAVE THE ANOINTING OF GOD:

Chapter Three of this course explained the importance of the anointing of God. You need this anointing to be successful in ministry.

FACE PROBLEMS AND DECISIONS:

Refusing to face problems and decisions leads to failure. Confront problems promptly and make decisions wisely using the strategies you learned in this course.

KNOW YOUR PURPOSE:

God has a specific purpose for each believer. Knowing your purpose involves having spiritual vision, a knowledge of why you exist and what God has called you to do. (You can learn more about this in the Harvestime International Institute course, *"Management By Objectives."*)

A man with a vision does not live in the past, fretting over mistakes and failures or gloating over success. A vision and clear knowledge of purpose helps you focus on the future. As Paul said:

> **Brethren, I count not myself to have apprehended: but this one thing I do, forgetting those things which are behind, and reaching forth unto those things which are before... (Philippians 3:13)**

HAVE A PLAN:

You will never achieve your purpose unless you have a plan to do so. You can learn how to plan in the Harvestime International Institute course, *"Management By Objectives."*

IMPLEMENT THE PLAN:

Having a good plan is not enough to achieve your purpose in ministry. You must also implement the plan. You must be able to organize, delegate, and supervise. One test of good spiritual leadership is whether or not it results in the successful achievement of God's purposes and plans. You can learn how to do this in the Harvestime International Institute course entitled *"Management By Objectives."*

LIVE A HOLY LIFE:

You will only be successful in ministry if you live a holy life, meeting the qualifications for leaders discussed in Chapter Four of this course. Sin guarantees failure. Holiness assures success.

He that covereth this sins shall not prosper; but whoso confesseth and forsaketh them shall have mercy. (Proverbs 28:13)

SEEK WISDOM FROM GOD:

Human wisdom is not sufficient to make good decisions and lead others. You must have wisdom from God to be a successful leader:

If any of you lack wisdom, let him ask of God, that giveth to all men liberally, and upbraideth not; and it shall be given him. (James 1:5)

STRIVE FOR EXCELLENCE:

Do not settle for "good enough." Strive for excellence:

...Approve things that are excellent. (Philippians 1:10)

DO ALL FOR GOD'S GLORY:

If you do everything for God's glory instead of your own, you will be successful:

And whatsoever you do in word or deed, do all in the name of the Lord Jesus, giving thanks to God... (Colossians 3:17)

SEEK FIRST THE KINGDOM:

You will be successful if the Kingdom of God is your priority:

But seek ye first the Kingdom of God and His righteousness; and all these things (including success) shall be added unto you. (Matthew 6:33)

Kingdom priorities can be set through proper organization. (See Acts 6:1-7.)

FOLLOW THE EXAMPLE:

As you learned in this course, Jesus is the example of the greatest spiritual leader. Jesus said:

For I have given you an example, that ye should do as I have done to you. (John 13:15)

When you compare yourself to anything other than the example of Christ, it is not good. Jacob compared Joseph to his brothers and set in motion events motivated by jealousy and hatred. The people of Israel compared themselves to other nations and adopted their wicked ways. Saul heard a comparison of himself to David and was poisoned by jealousy.

Comparison may be useful to stretch your vision and challenge you to fulfill your potential. But another person's achievements are not the standard for your life. Your success is not measured in relation to the performance of others. For this reason Peter's question to the Lord about John, "Lord, what about this man," received the rebuke, "What is that to you? You follow me." (John 21:21-22).

DECISION, DISCIPLINE, DIRECTION, DETERMINATION

Actually, success can be easily summarized in one statement:

> Follow the example of Jesus in decision, discipline, direction, and determination.

The Apostle Paul did this:

> **Know ye not that they which run in a race run all, but one receiveth the prize? So run, that ye may obtain.**
>
> **And every man that striveth for the mastery is temperate in all things. Now they do it to obtain a corruptible crown; but we an incorruptible.**
>
> **I therefore so run, not as uncertainly; so fight I, not as one that beateth the air;**
>
> **But I keep under my body, and bring it into subjection; lest that by any means, when I have preached to others, I myself should be a castaway. (I Corinthians 9:24-27)**

Paul made a decision. He wanted to be successful. He wanted to win the "race" of life (Verse 24). To do this, he realized he must be disciplined, which means to be temperate in all things (Verses 25 and 27). He had direction. He did not run or fight aimlessly. He was not uncertain about his purpose or plans (Verse 26). He was also determined to obtain, to be successful (Verses 24-25).

THE PRICE OF SUCCESS

Are you willing to pay the price of success? Here it is:

> **But he that knew not, and did commit things worthy of stripes, shall be beaten with few stripes. For unto whomsoever much is given, of him shall be much required; and to whom men have committed much, of him they will ask the more. (Luke 12:48)**

The more successful you are, the more God requires of you. This is the price of success.

SELF-TEST

1. Write the Key Verse from memory.

____

____

____

2. Define success.

____

____

____

3. How does success in God's Kingdom differs from that of the world?

____

____

____

4. Summarize the basic principles of success which you learned in this lesson.

____

____

____

(Answers to tests are provided at the conclusion of the final chapter in this manual.)

FOR FURTHER STUDY

This lesson covered some basic principles of success. There are many other success principles recorded in God's Word. This section will help you continue your study of these principles.

1. During the next year, read through the entire Bible. Mark every commandment that is given. Keeping these commandments will assure a successful life and ministry (Joshua 1:8).

2. The Appendix of this course explains how to study the lives of leaders whose stories are told in the Bible. Study the lives of leaders who were successful. Identify the things which made them successful and incorporate these into your own life.

3. Read the book of Ecclesiastes which describes worldly "success." Especially note Chapter 2. The person who bases success on such standards is left empty and unhappy. The person who bases his prosperity on God's standards is content and happy. Read the conclusion in Ecclesiastes 12:13-14.

4. The books of I and II Timothy and Titus were written to young men in leadership positions in ministry. Study these books carefully and list the principles of success which the Apostle Paul shares.

5. Remember this: "It is better to try and fail than to do nothing and succeed." You never fail until you say, "I Quit!"

6. Finances are very important to successful ministry. You need money in order to accomplish God's work. Here are some Scriptural principles of financial success:

   God is your source: Genesis 22:14.

   God wants you to be financially successful: Psalms 35:27; 23:1; Mark 12:43-44; Ephesians 3:29; Galatians 3:13; I Timothy 6:17; III John 2

   If you put God's Kingdom first, He will supply your needs: Matthew 6:33

   Financial success is a reward for:

   -Giving God priority: Proverbs 3:9-10; Matthew 6:33
   -Loving God: Proverbs 8:21
   -Giving God the glory: Proverbs 10:22
   -Desiring to be godly: Proverbs 13:21; 15:6
   -Humility: Proverbs 22:4
   -Readiness to give: Proverbs 22:9

-Trusting God: Proverbs 28:25
-Liberal sowing: Proverbs 11:24-25; Luke 6:38; II Corinthians 9:6,10

God gives you the power to get wealth: Deuteronomy 8:18-19

Wealth is the result of work:

-Diligent work: Proverbs 10;4; 13:4
-Intelligent work: Proverbs 10:5
-Honest work: Proverbs 13:11
-Quiet work: Proverbs 14:23

Giving makes you financially successful. You are to give:

-First to the Lord: Malachi 3:1-2; Proverbs 3:9-10
-Cheerfully: II Corinthians 9:7
-Willingly: Exodus 25:2; I Chronicles 29:9; II Corinthians 8:12
-Freely: Ezra 2:68
-According to your ability: Matthew 5:42; Acts 11:29; II Corinthians 8:12; Deuteronomy 16:17; Ezra 2:69
-For God's glory: Matthew 6:3
-With simplicity: Romans 12:8
-To the poor: Proverbs 3:27-28; 19:17; 21:13; 28:27
-Secretly: Matthew 6:3
-Regularly: I Corinthians 16:2
-By percentage of income: Genesis 14:20; 28:22; Leviticus 27:30; II Chronicles 31:5; Malachi 3:10

To be financially successful you must avoid:

-The love of money: I Timothy 6:10
-Trusting in riches: Psalms 49:6; I Chronicles 29:14
-Debt: Romans 13:8
-Laziness: Proverbs 6:6-11; 24:30-34
-Self-indulgence: Proverbs 13:18; 21:17; 23:21
-Dreaming: Proverbs 13:4
-Violence: 1:10-19
-Fraud: James 5:3-4; Proverbs 20:23; 13:11; 22:16
-Cheating: Proverbs 10:2
-Bribery: Proverbs 14:27
-Dishonesty: Acts 5:3-4; Proverbs 21:6
-Schemes to "get rich quick": Proverbs 28:20
-Borrowing and not repaying: Psalms 37:21
-Guaranteeing other people's debts: Proverbs 6:1; 11:15; 22:26

-Poor personal habits: Proverbs 23:21
-Lack of submission which affects financial success: Proverbs 13:18
-Hoarding money: Proverbs 10:22; I Timothy 6:10
-Not paying fair wages: Jeremiah 22:13
-Greed: Proverbs 28:22
-Refusing God's instruction: Proverbs 13:18
-Receiving large offerings for personal gain: I Samuel 2:29
-Withheld offerings: Proverbs 11:24

You will mature spiritually to the degree you are faithful in giving: Luke 16:11

7. The Book of Proverbs contains some of the greatest success principles in the entire Bible. Read one chapter each day and you can read the book through once each month. Mark the success principles in your Bible and meditate on them. Incorporate them into your life and ministry.

8. Here are some direct Scriptural references to success and prosperity:

-Deuteronomy 29:9
-Joshua 1:8-9
-II Chronicles 31:21; 32:30
-I Kings 2:3
-Nehemiah 1:11; 2:20
-Psalms 1:3; 73:12; 122:6
-Proverbs 28:13
-Ecclesiastes 7:14; 11:6
-Isaiah 54:17; 55:11
-III John 2

9. Hezekiah had a four-point plan of success. He...

-Trusted in the Lord.
-Held fast to Him (close relationship).
-Followed Him.
-Kept His commandments.

Because of this, he was successful in everything he did.

CHAPTER THIRTEEN

COUNTING THE COST

OBJECTIVES:

Upon completion of this chapter you will be able to:

- Write the Key Verse from memory.
- Summarize three aspects of the cost of leadership.
- Identify the true test of spiritual leadership.

KEY VERSE:

> **Then said Jesus unto His disciples, If any man will come after me, let him deny himself, and take up his cross, and follow me. (Matthew 16:24)**

INTRODUCTION

In this course you have learned about management of spiritual resources through proper leadership. You have learned how to be a good steward and lead like a servant and shepherd.

You learned of the qualifications and tasks of leaders, the importance of the anointing and how to make decisions and solve problems. You studied principles of success and were warned of things that result in failure. You also learned how to train leaders and followers.

Only one question remains: Are you prepared to pay the high cost of serving as a spiritual leader?

COUNTING THE COST

Jesus stressed the importance of counting the cost before you make spiritual decisions. He used two natural examples, those of a man building a tower and a king going to war:

> **For which of you, intending to build a tower, sitteth not down first, and counteth the cost, whether he have sufficient to finish it?**
>
> **Lest haply, after he hath laid the foundation, and is not able to finish it, all that behold it begin to mock him.**

Saying, This man began to build, and was not able to finish.

Or what king, going to make war against another king, sitteth not down first, and consulteth whether he be able with ten thousand to meet him that cometh against him with twenty thousand?

Or else, while, the other is yet a great way off, he sendeth an ambassage, and desireth conditions of peace. (Luke 14:28-32)

By these examples Jesus illustrated the importance of counting the costs before you make a spiritual commitment. Just what are the costs of serving as a spiritual leader?

THREE ASPECTS OF LEADERSHIP

Read Luke 9:57-62 in your Bible. In this passage three men approached Jesus wanting to be disciples. To each of these potential disciples, Jesus reveals a different aspect of the costs of spiritual leadership:

CONSIDERED COSTS: (Luke 9:57-58)

The first man attempts to become a disciple through self-effort. He does not wait to be called by Jesus. Like discipleship, leadership is not an offer man makes to God. It is a call of God to man. If you try to lead by self-effort, you will fail. You must be called and anointed of God. Jesus said to this man, "If you follow me, this is what you will face." The costs of leadership include sacrifice as well as service:

Hereby perceive we the love of God, because He laid down His life for us; and we ought to lay down our lives for the brethren. (I John 3:16)

The cost of leadership includes loneliness. The Apostle Paul wrote:

This thou knowest, that all they which are in Asia be turned away from me... (II Timothy 1:15)

A leader often experiences rejection and criticism:

He (Jesus) came unto His own, and His own received Him not. (John 1:11

A leader may also experience persecution. Read of the terrible things Paul experienced in II Corinthians 11:23-27.

A leader has many duties:

Beside those things that are without, that which cometh upon me daily, the care of all the churches. (II Corinthians 11:28)

A leader must be disciplined:

But I keep under my body, and bring it into subjection: lest that by any means, when I have preached to others, I myself should be a castaway. (I Corinthians 9:27)

A leader has a great responsibility to walk worthy of his spiritual calling:

Therefore seeing we have this ministry, as we have received mercy, we faint not;

But have renounced the hidden things of dishonesty, not walking in craftiness, nor handling the word of God deceitfully; but by manifestation of the truth commending ourselves to every man's conscience in the sight of God. (II Corinthians 4:1-2)

I therefore, the prisoner of the Lord, beseech you that ye walk worthy of the vocation wherewith ye are called. (Ephesians 4:1)

PROPER PRIORITIES: (Luke 9:59-60)

The second man was called by Jesus to "follow." As you have learned, to "follow" means to come after one that goes before, to imitate an example. It involves both belief and obedience.

When Jesus called His 12 disciples, He told them to come and follow. He did not outline a career path. He did not give them details of the program. The disciple had to leave the old life behind because of the call alone. What decisions, partings, and sacrifices this might require remain unknown.

The leader is a follower who must leave a life of security for one of insecurity in the eyes of the world. The commitment is not to a program, but to a person. That person is the Lord Jesus Christ. In the Luke passage, the response of this man to the call to follow was "suffer me first...." He wanted to follow Jesus, but it was not his priority.

Jesus would never suggest that a person ignore the needs of his parents (see John 19:25-27). It is a matter of priorities which is stressed in this story. This man said he wanted to "bury his father" first. In Old Testament times when a person said he was waiting to "bury his father," it did not necessarily mean his father had died. It meant he was waiting until his father died in order to receive the inheritance that rightfully belonged to him. So, when this man used this excuse, he was placing his future inheritance before the call of the Lord Jesus Christ. At the critical moment when Jesus calls a man to follow Him and become a leader, nothing must be placed before that call.

In another passage, Jesus explained in more detail the importance of proper priorities:

> **Then said Jesus unto His disciples, If any man will come after me, let him deny himself, and take up his cross, and follow me. (Matthew 16:24)**

Self-denial must come before we can take up the cross. The old selfish and sinful nature must be denied. (Read Romans 7-8 about Paul's struggle in this area.) When self has died, the cross must become your priority. The cross is symbolic of the sacrifice, pain, rejection, insult, and hardship involved in doing God's will. The cross may even mean a call to death by martyrdom for the sake of the Gospel.

"Taking up the cross" does not refer to the burdens of life. These are common to all men. They are the afflictions, trials, disappointments, and depression that come to us because of living in a sinful world. The believer is not excluded from such burdens of life. He experiences illness, accidents, fire, and natural hazards because he lives in a world marred by sin. But these burdens are not "taking up the cross." Cross bearing is voluntary, not something imposed by the burdens of life. It is a continuous (daily) choosing to deny the desires of self in order to do God's will.

Jesus said, "Whosoever doth not bear his cross and come after me, cannot be my disciple." Taking up the cross is not pleasing to human nature because it involves self denial. It must be done voluntarily for the sake of Christ.

To take up the cross, you must empty your hands of the things of the world. If your heart is set on money and material things, your hands are too full to take up the cross. If your time is consumed by pleasure and things that please the flesh, your hands are too full to take up the cross. After denying self and taking up the cross, the next step is to follow. You must leave behind the old lifestyle and sinful relationships.

You will never become a leader by sitting and waiting for it to happen. <u>YOU</u> must take the first steps: Deny yourself, take up your cross, and follow. Matthew could have remained at the tax table and Peter at his nets. They could both have pursued their trades honestly and might have enjoyed spiritual experiences. But if they wanted to become spiritual leaders, they had to leave the old situation and enter the new. Matthew left the tax tables and Peter left his nets.

This does not mean everyone must leave his present job and home to become a leader. What it does mean is that it will require a change in lifestyle. In some cases it may also mean leaving home, jobs and loved ones for the sake of the Gospel. You must follow wherever Jesus leads.

Proper priorities means you must forsake all else to accept this call:

So likewise, whosoever he be of you that forsaketh not all that he hath, he cannot be my disciple. (Luke 14:33)

Serving others must become a priority:

But it shall not be so among you: but whosoever will be great among you, let him be your minister:

And whosoever will be chief among you, let him be your servant;

Even as the Son of man came not to be ministered unto, but to minister, and to give His life a ransom for many. (Matthew 20:26-28)

The Kingdom of God must become your main priority:

Therefore take no thought, saying, What shall we eat? or What shall we drink? or, Wherewithal shall we be clothed?...

But seek ye first the Kingdom of God, and His righteousness; and all these things shall be added unto you. (Matthew 6:31,33)

ABSOLUTE AIMS: (Luke 9:61-62)

The third man in Luke 9:57-62 wanted to follow, but he wanted to do so on his own terms. Bidding his family farewell was a normal thing to do, but Jesus had called him. What was his real aim in life? Did he want to become a leader or to follow his own plan for life? This man's aims in life were not settled. He was holding back, torn between the old life and the new to which Jesus called. His absolute aim in life was not the call of God. Your commitment to leadership must be complete. It must become the absolute aim of your life.

THE TRUE TEST OF SPIRITUAL LEADERSHIP

The true test of leadership is what happens when you are no longer present with your followers. Do they continue to be faithful to what you have taught them? Do they teach others what they have learned? Can they continue to mature spiritually without your physical presence? If so, you have passed the true test of spiritual leadership.

A FINAL CHALLENGE

Always remember your great responsibility as a leader:

A disciple is not above his teacher (leader), but everyone when he is fully taught will be like his teacher. (Luke 6:40) Revised Standard Version

Do not be discouraged by problems with followers. Jesus experienced such problems. On one occasion, Peter, James and John displayed a hateful attitude by wanting to call fire from heaven to destroy an unreceptive Samaritan village (Luke 9:51-55). Peter denied the Lord three times (Luke 22:54-62). All three were asleep in the Garden of Gethsemane when they were told to pray (Luke 22:45-46).

But this handful of followers were worth the investment of time and ministry by Jesus. They proved to be faithful men, despite their faults and failures. Through them, the Gospel spread throughout the nations of the world. If you are willing to pay the high costs to serve as a spiritual leader, is it possible that you, too, can be used of God to raise up such committed followers?

> I heard a call "come follow"...that was all.
> Earth's joys grew dim;
> My soul went after Him.
> I rose and followed...that was all.

SELF-TEST

1. Write the Key Verse from memory.

____

____

____

2. What were the three aspects of the cost of leadership discussed in this lesson?

____

____

____

3. What is the true test of spiritual leadership?

____

____

____

(Answers to tests are provided at the conclusion of the final chapter in this manual.)

FOR FURTHER STUDY

1. Study the following references and consider what it cost each of these men to serve in a leadership position:

   Joseph: Genesis 37-50

   Moses: The book of Exodus

   Hosea: The book of Hosea

   Ezekiel: Ezekiel 3

   The Apostle Paul: Acts 9-28

2. Now that you have finished this study of management, we suggest you obtain the Harvestime International Institute courses *"Environmental Analysis"* and *"Management By Objectives."*

   These courses will add to your understanding of the leadership, planning, and organization necessary for effective ministry.

APPENDIX

This Appendix provides opportunity for you to learn more about management principles by studying the lives of important characters in the Bible.

A "biography" is the story of someone's life. When you study the life of an important person in the Bible, you are doing a "biographical study." By studying the lives of Bible characters you can learn from their experiences. The Bible states:

> **Now all these things happened unto them for ensamples; and they are written for our admonition. (I Corinthians 10:11)**

Events which happened in the lives of Bible characters were recorded for your benefit. Their experiences can teach you great spiritual lessons about leadership. By observing their failures as leaders you can learn of errors to avoid. By observing their success as leaders you can develop positive leadership qualities in your own life.

Here are four steps to follow when doing a biographical study:

STEP ONE: Select The Person To Be Studied

You may choose a person that is of special interest to you. You may want to select a person from the lists given in Hebrews 11, Galatians 3:7, or Luke 4:27. You might study a person in a certain book of the Bible which you are presently reading.

Remember that the greatest leader of all was Jesus Christ. You may want to study His life first as a perfect example of a leader.

When you select a person to study, be careful not to confuse names. For example, there are some 30 Zachariahs in the Bible, 20 Nathans, 15 Jonathans, 8 Judases, 7 Marys, 5 James, and 5 Johns. Be sure all the verses you study are about the person you have selected and not another individual with the same name.

Some people also have more than one name. For example, in the Old Testament Jacob's name was changed to Israel and Abram's name was changed to Abraham. In the New Testament, Saul's name was changed to Paul.

STEP TWO: Gather The Information

Read everything the Bible records about the person you are studying. If you have Bible reference books available, use these for additional information. For example, if you have a concordance you can look up the name of the person and find a list of all references to him/her in the Bible.

If you do not have a concordance, gather the references directly from the Bible. Most references about a person are found within one book or a series of consecutive Bible books. List all the references about the person, then read and study each reference.

STEP THREE: Analyze The Information

The following list identifies some of the information you should gather as you study. The Bible may not contain information on all of these items in every case, but try to include everything it does reveal about the person you are studying. Look for this biographical information:

Name and meaning of name.

Relatives: Parents, brothers and sisters, ancestors, children.

Birth: Location, importance of birth, unusual events surrounding birth.

Childhood and early training.

Geographical setting: Where does the story of this person's life occur?

Friends and associates, personal relationships.

Occupation or vocation: What position or office did they occupy? How did they earn their living?

Physical description.

Positive character and leadership traits.

Negative character and leadership traits.

Significant events:

First encounter with God.

Conversion.

Call to service.

Greatest crisis or turning point in the person's life.

Ways they succeeded as a leader: What caused their success?

Ways they failed as a leader: What caused their failure? What was the result? What did they do about it?

Death: When, where, unusual circumstances.

STEP FOUR: Apply What You Learn

Apply what you learn about this person to your own life:

1. What were their positive traits as a leader? Ask God to help you develop them in your own life.

2. What were their negative traits? Do you see any of these in your own life? Ask God to help you overcome them.

3. In what ways did this person succeed as a leader? Are you applying these principles of success?

4. In what ways did this person fail as a leader? Are these problems to you also? What will you do to change?

5. Compose one sentence which summarizes the greatest principle of leadership you learned from this person's life. For example, a statement about the life of Samson might be "Spiritual compromise results in failure."

   Here is an example of a biographical study:

EXAMPLE: A BIOGRAPHICAL STUDY

STEP ONE: Select The Person To Be Studied

King Saul

STEP TWO: Gather The Information

The story of Saul is found in I Samuel 9-31. The information on Saul was gathered from these chapters.

STEP THREE: Analyze The Information

Name and meaning of name: Saul. Meaning "Asked of God." I Samuel 9:2

Relatives: Parents, brothers and sisters, ancestors, children:

Saul was the son of Kish who was the son of Abiel, the son of Zeror, the son of Bechorath, the son of Aphiah. Kish was a Benjamite and a mighty man of power. I Samuel 9:1 . Saul had three sons: Jonathan, Ishui, and Melchishula. He had two daughters, Merab and Michal. His wife's name was Ahinoam: I Samuel 14:49-50

Birth: Location, importance of birth, unusual events surrounding birth: The Bible does not state these facts.

Childhood and early training: Cared for his father asses: I Samuel 9:3

Geographical setting: Judah

Friends and associates, personal relationships:

The children of Belial despised him: I Samuel 10:27. He was close to Abner, the captain of his host, who was his uncle's son: I Samuel 14:50. David became an associate of Saul. At first he was in Saul's favor, then Saul became jealous and their relationship was broken: I Samuel 18:6-9. When Saul first became king he had a band of men whose "hearts God had touched." When Saul started adding "strong and valiant" men without direction from God, his problems began: I Samuel 10:26; 13:2; 14:52.

Occupation or vocation: First king of Israel.

Physical description: From his shoulders upward he was higher than any of the people: I Samuel 9:2, 10:23. He was described as "goodly" which means handsome: I Samuel 9:2

Positive leadership traits:

-Showed concern for family:	I Samuel 9:5
-"Choice man":	I Samuel 9:2; 10:24
-Let spirit change his heart:	I Samuel 10:6; 11:6
-Modest (Hid among the baggage):	I Samuel 10:22
-Refuses to execute vengeance:	I Samuel 11
-Leadership (Rallied people):	I Samuel 11
-Man of the spirit:	I Samuel 11
-Originally was obedient:	I Samuel 9:27
-Aligned himself with godly:	I Samuel 10:26; 11:7
-Bold for God:	I Samuel 10:6
-Originally was humble:	I Samuel 9:21

Negative leadership traits:

Did what seemed necessary rather than obeying God: I Samuel 13:8-13

Disobeyed and lied, then refused to accept the blame: I Samuel 15
Grieved God's people: I Samuel 15:35
More concerned with what man thought than God: I Samuel 15:30
Chose strong and valiant men to be close to him rather than the band of men God had touched: I Samuel 10:26; 14:52
Fearful: I Samuel 17:11
Judged by outward appearances: I Samuel 17:33
Trusted the armor of man: I Samuel 17:38
Jealous: I Samuel 18:6-9
Evil spirit: I Samuel 18:10
Spirit of revenge: I Samuel 18:11
Plotted against God's anointed: I Samuel 18:20-30

Significant events:

First encounter with God:	I Samuel 9:15-27
Conversion:	I Samuel 10:9
Call to service:	I Samuel 10:1

Greatest crisis or turning point in the person's life: Disobeyed and the kingdom was taken from him. I Samuel 13

Death: When, where, unusual circumstances. Saul died by his own hand. His three sons, his armor bearer and all his men died the same day in Mt. Gilboa during a battle with the Philistines. I Samuel 31

STEP FOUR: Apply What You Learn

Positive leadership traits in Saul's life which I should seek to develop in my own life:

When the Spirit of the Lord comes on a person he can be changed into "another man": I Samuel 10:6. I should seek that type of anointing from God.

Negative leadership traits in Saul's life which I should seek to avoid in my own life:

God desires leaders after His own heart: I Samuel 13:14. Although Saul failed in this area, I desire to be such a leader. Disobedience: Doing what is easy or seems necessary rather than what God commands. Placing blame on others for my own sin. Caring more what man thinks than what God thinks of me. I would do well to review the entire list of Saul's negative traits and examine my own heart from time to time.

God's call was for Saul to be captain over the people: I Samuel 10:1. It was people who made him king instead (I Samuel 12:12-15; 10:24). God was to be Israel's king. I should be cautious that the praise of people does not turn me from God's plan and make me what I should not be.

Although God was originally with Saul (I Samuel 10:7,9; 13:14), he later lost the kingdom. It is important to note that even after Saul's sin and the prophecy of losing the kingdom, God's anointing still rested on Saul (I Samuel 14:47). The gifts and callings of God are without repentance. Saul still heard God's voice (I Samuel 15:1) and worshiped Him (15:31), but he had unconfessed sin and lost the kingdom. David recognized the danger of touching a man anointed by God as a leader. I should heed this warning.

The greatest truth learned from the life of Saul is the results of disobedience to God. It is summarized in the statement of Samuel: "Behold to obey is better than sacrifice, and to hearken than the fat of rams" (I Samuel 15:22). The results of such disobedience is summarized in David's statement about Saul: "How the mighty are fallen" (II Samuel 1:19).

Note: On the following pages are forms for you to reproduce and use in studying Bible leaders.

BIOGRAPHICAL STUDY OF BIBLE LEADERS

STEP ONE: Select The Person To Be Studied

"The leader I will study is:___________ "

STEP TWO: Gather The Information

List the Bible references which record the life of this person:

STEP THREE: Analyze The Information

Name and meaning of name:

Relatives: Parents, brothers and sisters, ancestors, children:

Birth: Location, importance of birth, unusual events surrounding birth:

Childhood and early training:

Geographical setting:

Friends and associates, personal relationships:

Occupation or vocation:

Physical description:

Positive leadership traits:

Negative leadership traits:

Significant events:

First encounter with God:

Conversion:

Call to service:

Greatest crisis or turning point:

Death: When, where, unusual circumstances.

STEP FOUR: Apply What You Learn

"I can apply what I learned about ____________to my own life in the following ways:"

ANSWERS TO SELF-TESTS

CHAPTER ONE:

1. To aspire to leadership is an honorable ambition. (I Timothy 3:1) New English Bible

2. "Management" is another word for "stewardship." Stewards, or managers, are responsible over something entrusted to them by someone else. Management is the process of accomplishing God's purposes and plans through proper use of human, material, and spiritual resources. Good management is measured by whether or not such plans and purposes are accomplished.

3. The resources are the Gospel, finances, material resources of ministry, spiritual gifts, and other believers.

4. Faithfulness.

5. Jesus Christ.

6. Compare your summary to that given in Chapter One.

7. Compare your answer to the summary in Chapter One.

CHAPTER TWO:

1. And He gave some apostles; and some, prophets; and some, evangelists; and some, pastors, and teachers. (Ephesians 4:11)

2. 2, 1, 4, 3, 5, 6, 7

3. -Elders
   -Deacons
   -Bishops

CHAPTER THREE:

1. But my horn shalt thou exalt like the horn of an unicorn; I shall be anointed with fresh oil. (Psalms 92:10)

2. To "anoint" means to dedicate or consecrate something or someone by applying oil.

3. Oil is a symbol of the Holy Spirit. Anointing a person with oil is symbolic of the Holy Spirit coming upon him for a specific purpose.

4. The leper's anointing for relationship; the priest's anointing for holiness; and the leader's anointing for position and power.

5. God is the source of anointing for ministry.

6. The anointing establishes your position in God, enables you to fulfill God's purposes, gives you wisdom to lead, and breaks the yokes of bondage in those to whom you minister.

7. God does not anoint on the basis of education, intelligence, abilities, or experience. He anoints on the basis of heart attitude.

8. Ungodly forces want to hinder you from walking in the anointing because they know it is anointed ministry which accomplishes God's purposes.

9. Because you will be ineffective and experience great difficulties if you do not do so.

10. By walking continually in the three types of anointing discussed in this lesson.

CHAPTER FOUR:

1. For we are His workmanship, created in Christ Jesus unto good works which God hath before ordained that we should walk in them. (Ephesians 2:10)

2. Qualifications are not natural abilities. They are qualities of character and conduct. Biblical qualifications for leadership are qualities of character and conduct described in God's Word as necessary for leaders. They are evidences of a godly lifestyle.

3. The fruit of evangelism is being a powerful witness of the Gospel message.
4. See the list of Christ-like qualities given in Chapter Four.

5. 9, 7, 8, 5, 6, 2, 4, 3, 1

6. The passages are I Timothy 3 and Titus 1.

7. That they be born again, baptized in the Holy Spirit, have a specific call and anointing from God to be a leader, and be spiritually mature.

CHAPTER FIVE:

1. Let this mind be in you, which was also in Christ Jesus;

   Who, being in the form of God, thought it not robbery to be equal with God;

   But made Himself of no reputation, and took upon Him the form of a servant, and was made in the likeness of men. (Philippians 4:5-7)

2. Servant leadership.

3. Jesus Christ.

4. The power in servanthood is that it reduces a person and humbles him to the point that he can be used for God. This is illustrated in the life of Jesus.

5. Secular leaders have dominion over their followers, they exercise authority over them, and act as chiefs and lords.

6. We serve the Body of Christ and lost and dying humanity. In reality, our service is unto the Lord.

7. Compare your explanation to the discussion in Chapter Five.

CHAPTER SIX:

1. Feed the flock of God which is among you, taking the oversight thereof, not by constraint, but willingly; not for filthy lucre, but of a ready mind;

   Neither as being lords over God's heritage, but being ensamples to the flock. (I Peter 5:2-3)

2. Jesus Christ.

3. All true believers in Jesus are part of the one sheepfold.

4. Compare your discussion to that in Chapter Six.

5. Compare your discussion to that in Chapter Six.

CHAPTER SEVEN:

1. And He (God) gave some apostles; and some, prophets; and some, evangelists; and some, pastors and teachers;

   For the perfecting of the saints for the work of the ministry, for the edifying of the body of Christ. (Ephesians 4:11-12)

2. Perfecting believers for the work of the ministry.

3. To perfect is to prepare or equip believers for the work of the ministry. It involves teaching, preaching, demonstrating, training, and mobilizing.

4. The results when believers are properly "perfected" for the work of the ministry include:

   -The work of the ministry is done: Ephesians 4:12
   -The Body of Christ (the Church) is edified (built up): Ephesians 4:12)
   -People reach spiritual maturity: Ephesians 4:13-15
   -Unity results: Ephesians 4:13
   -People are conformed into the image of Christ: Ephesians 4:13
   -People become stable doctrinally, grounded in the truth: Ephesians 4:15-16
   -The Body of Christ functions effectively: Ephesians 4:16

5. Compare your discussion to that in Chapter Seven.

CHAPTER EIGHT:

1. A man's heart deviseth his way; but the Lord directeth his steps. (Proverbs 16:9)

2. The Biblical approach is not voting or "majority rule." God sets leaders in the church to make decisions.

3. Compare your summary to the guidelines given in Chapter Eight.

4. A model for decision-making is an example to follow when making choices.

5. A model provides an example for you to follow.

CHAPTER NINE:

1. All Scripture is given by inspiration of God, and is profitable for doctrine, for reproof, for correction, for instruction in righteousness:

   That the man of God may be perfect, thoroughly furnished unto all good works. (II Timothy 3:16-17)

2. Compare your summary to that given in Chapter Nine.

3. Compare your summary to that given in Chapter Nine.

4. Compare your list of reasons to those listed in Chapter Nine.

5. Compare your summary to that given in Chapter Nine.

6. Because of spiritually immature and carnal Christians motivated by Satan, flesh, and pride.

7. When we discipline and solve conflicts on the basis of God's Word, people are perfected and equipped for the work of the ministry. God's Word is effective for discipline, reproof, and correction.

CHAPTER TEN:

1. A disciple is not above his teacher, but everyone when he is fully taught will be like his teacher. (Luke 6:40) Revised Standard Version

2. Training others is an important responsibility because those you train will become like you.

3. We train leaders and followers for the purpose of going to all nations, teaching them the Gospel, baptizing them, and then guiding them on to spiritual maturity through further teaching.

4. -Depend on God.
   -Make it a matter of prayer.
   -Take the initiative.
   -Look at potential, not problems.
   -Make the costs clear.
   -Select those who meet basic requirements.

5. -Association
-Instruction
-Demonstration
-Consecration
-Participation
-Vision
-Supervision
-Delegation

6. The Ephesus model.

CHAPTER ELEVEN:

1. A just man falleth seven times, and riseth up again. Proverbs 24:16

2. For a list of those who turned failure to success see the discussion in Chapter Eleven.

3. For a list of those whose lives ended in failure see the discussion in Chapter Eleven.

4. -Revealing
-Repenting
-Returning
-Restoring

5. Failure in relationship and because of acts of commission or omission.

CHAPTER TWELVE:

1. This book of the law shall not depart out of thy mouth; but thou shalt meditate therein day and night, that thou mayest observe to do according to all that is written therein; for then thou shalt make thy way prosperous, and then thou shalt have good success. (Joshua 1:8)

2. In God's Kingdom, success is the maximum use of one's gifts and abilities within the range of responsibilities given by God. You are successful when you properly use your spiritual resources for the work of God.

3. Compare your explanation to the discussion in Chapter Twelve.

4. Compare your summary to the discussion in Chapter Twelve.

CHAPTER THIRTEEN:

1. Then said Jesus unto His disciples, If any man will come after me, let him deny himself,

and take up his cross, and follow me. (Matthew 16:24)

2. Three important aspects of the costs of leadership are considered costs, proper priorities, and absolute aims.

3. The true test of leadership is what happens when you are no longer present with those you have led. Do they continue to be faithful to what you have taught them? Do they teach others what they have learned? Can they continue to mature spiritually without your physical presence?

CPSIA information can be obtained
at www.ICGtesting.com
Printed in the USA
FSHW020815191121
86198FS